RAMS, ROMS, & Robots

The Inside Story of Computers

A scientist holds a microchip containing 150,000 transistors. Its circuitry is shown on a 20- by 20-foot computer printout behind him.

*James Jespersen
and Jane Fitz-Randolph*

RAMS, ROMS, & Robots

The Inside Story of Computers

ILLUSTRATED WITH DIAGRAMS

BY BRUCE HISCOCK

AND WITH PHOTOGRAPHS

Atheneum   1984   New York

ACKNOWLEDGMENT
The authors wish to thank R. Gregg Merrill
for reading the manuscript
and making many helpful suggestions.

Library of Congress Cataloging in Publication Data

Jespersen, James.
RAMS, ROMS, and robots.

Includes index.
SUMMARY: An examination of computers, how they work,
their strengths and limitations, their many uses, and
their future potential.
1. Computers—Juvenile literature. [1. Computers]
I. Fitz-Randolph, Jane. II. Title.
QA76.23.J47 1984   001.64   84-3001
ISBN 0-689-31063-3

Published simultaneously in Canada by
McClelland & Stewart, Ltd.
Composition by
Yankee Typesetters, Concord, New Hampshire
Printed and bound by
Fairfield Graphics, Fairfield, Pennsylvania
Designed by Mary Ahern
First Edition

For Jodelle Christine

CONTENTS

RAMS, ROMS, & Robots

The Inside Story of Computers

INTRODUCTION

A cartoon in a computer magazine showed two scientists standing in front of a large computer. Piles of punched paper on the floor suggested that the machine had been grinding away for hours—"number crunching," as computer scientists call it. Inspecting a segment of the tape, one scientist solemnly reports to the other, "It says the answer is one."

We laugh without knowing why. What's so funny? Probably it's the idea of an awesome machine slaving away heroically, only to come up with the simple answer "one." If the scientist said, "It says the answer is 4,720, 264.1952," the cartoon would not be funny. Somehow we feel we've received our money's worth if the answer is a big number that seems worthy of the machine's capabilities. Any second grader with a pad and pencil—or without a pad and pencil—could come up with the answer "one" in no time at all.

Of course, the real question is, What problem is "one" the answer to? If the problem is, "What is $\frac{1}{2}$ plus $\frac{1}{2}$?" then our amusement is justified. But if "one" is the answer to the problem "How many hours is it until the next big earthquake?" and we know that the computer has been dealing with thousands of bits of information from hundreds of sources, then the cartoon doesn't seem funny.

Many problems that appear to have simple answers are enormously complex: Will it rain tomorrow? If a salesman must visit seven specific cities once a week, how should he plan his route for the shortest driving distance? What is the best way to package one pound of assorted cookies into the smallest box possible? Questions like these are too complicated for the human mind to cope with. There are too many factors that contribute to the answer, too many variables to keep track of. As we shall see, in some versions of the traveling salesman problem, the biggest computer we have today wouldn't know the answer after fifteen billion years of computing—that's the estimated age of the universe. It appears, in fact, that there are some problems that no computer, no matter how big or fast, could ever solve.

But then there are other kinds of problems in which "what needs to be done" is very simple. It's just that it needs to be done thousands and millions of times, over and over—like computing the amount that should be withheld from paychecks for income taxes, or counting and summarizing census data.

Today's computers do much more than mere number crunching and digesting and summarizing data. They regulate our microwave ovens, control our cameras, let us play video games on our TV sets, and oversee the complex opera-

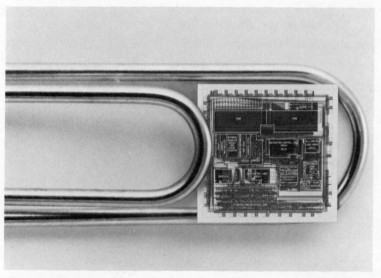

A complete computer on a single chip nestles comfortably on an ordinary paper clip.

tions of the world's communication systems. There are not enough people in the whole world to do what computers do, even if we all worked at it twenty-four hours a day.

Realizing how dependent we have become on computers is in some ways scary. But this is the price we pay to have "a slave at our elbow" that will perform our most monotonous tasks without complaining, or unscramble and interpret the faintest signals from our farthest spacecraft.

If our present-day computers seem awesome, how will we accept the prospect of "machines that think"? Several years ago inventors produced models of vacuum cleaners and lawn mowers that could be programmed to follow a certain pattern to clean a room or cut the grass perfectly without bumping into sofas or trees. But the public wasn't ready for such machines. We seem to be more comfortable in situations when we feel we are "in control."

Yet most people who saw the movie *Star Wars* had no trouble warming up to the robot R2-D2. Would it really be so bad to come home to your own R2-D2, who greeted you, "How was your day today? . . . By the way, I was monitoring television this morning and I taped a program on making popcorn balls I thought you might like. I also found that quotation you wanted to use in your science report. And, oh yes, Mary called and said she will meet you at seven this evening."

This conversation may seem like something we should expect only in science fiction movies, but many computer scientists believe that such robots are not only likely but inevitable. These developments are related to what is called "artificial intelligence"—the most fascinating and at the same time most disturbing branch of the whole field of computer science. So this book is about artificial intelligence as well as number crunching and counting and summarizing data. Let's begin at the beginning.

1.
Sticks and Stones

As I was going to St. Ives
I met a man with seven wives.
Each wife had seven sacks;
Each sack had seven cats;
Each cat had seven kits.
Kits, cats, sacks, wives—
How many were going to St. Ives?

Perhaps this was the question confronting the two scientists and their computer in our Introduction. The familiar old Mother Goose rhyme has been around for a long time; and anyone recalling his own first encounter with this peculiar group on the road to St. Ives doubtless remembers other childhood riddles, games, and verses having to do with counting. Whether numbering successful jumps in a rope-skipping contest, determining who was to be "it" in a game of kick-the-can, or parceling out M&Ms among friends, counting out the numbers in sing-song rhymes seemed to be part of the ritual and half the fun.

Counting, however, has always been much more than fun and games. Nobody knows how or when the idea of counting first developed, but certainly it's reasonable to suppose that one of the very earliest functions of language must have been a system of numbers. All languages do, in fact, include such systems. Counting is, like language itself, a basic achievement that sets man apart from animals. In spite of some remarkable feats that look like counting by a few trained horses and other animals in circuses and animal shows, even the smartest animals cannot count.

How did primitive peoples count? In the most natural, obvious, and universally available way possible—by using their fingers. Our words *digit* and *digital* come from the Latin word *digitus,* which means "finger." For really complicated calculations they could also use their toes. And probably parents and teachers didn't scold children for using their fingers in working problems. Instead, they taught them swift and clever ways to multiply and perform other calculations by using systems of "finger arithmetic" similar to sign language used by the deaf.

You yourself may have learned a simple system for multiplying numbers through the 10s without having to know the multiplication tables. To multiply 7×8, for example, you can simply fold down 7 minus 5, or 2 fingers on one hand; and 8 minus 5, or 3 fingers on the other. Then add the number of fingers folded down—$2 + 3 = 5$—and multiply those left standing—$3 \times 2 = 6$. The result is 5 tens plus 6 units, or 56.

Many variations of such systems are used all over the world today—often by people who cannot read or write, as was of course the case with primitive peoples. Some systems were introduced into Europe from Arab countries during the Middle Ages; others are used quite commonly for business transactions among Oriental peoples.

For working with numbers too large to be counted easily on fingers and toes—or to provide more permanent records—primitive peoples used pebbles for counting. Our word *calculate* comes from the Latin word *calculus,* meaning "pebble" or "small stone." By letting one pebble represent one sheep, a herdsman could keep track of the size of his flock in an easy, businesslike way. If a ewe gave birth to twin lambs, he added a couple of pebbles to his pile; if he withdrew a sheep to pay his taxes, he removed a stone from the pile. And so he knew just how many sheep he had at any time without having to go into the fields to count the flocks of milling, moving animals.

What did people count besides sheep and pebbles? All sorts of things. They counted goats, camels, and other domestic animals. They counted bags of grain and bales of hides. They counted numbers of warriors, chariots, and horses in their own and their enemies' armies; and they counted slaves and prisoners. They counted "summers" and "moons" to keep track of their own and their children's ages, and they counted the number of "suns" it took them to travel from one place to another, so that they could plan for next year's journey to an important festival or pow-wow.

One of the things it was most important to count was the cycles of various astronomical events. Charting the positions of stars and planets at different seasons provided information that guided travelers on their journeys across deserts and at sea; it also told them when to plant their crops in spring. Scholars believe that markings on a small bone found in France and dating back some thirty-five thousand years represent the waxing and waning of the moon. Of course, the ancient astronomer who inscribed this bone needed a far more sophisticated knowledge of mathematics than simple counting.

So did the early astronomers who laid out great computing devices in stone or wood, such as the mysterious Stonehenge in southern England. The priests who planned and "read" these devices could predict eclipses and other astronomical events with great accuracy; doubtless they commanded the respect of other tribe members just as computer experts who use computers to predict stock market futures and election results do today.

Probably one of the earliest forms of this kind of primitive computing was the simple sundial. It may have been a lone tree on an open plain, or a pinnacle of rocks. As the shadow of the tree or rock crept in its circular path along the ground, it traced out the motion of the sun in its daily trip across the sky. We might say that the sundial's shadow *imitated* the apparent motion of the sun. Or even that the sundial represented a small *model* of the sun's motion. We could say the same thing about a clock; the motion of the hands across the clock's face is in a way a small model of the movement of the sun.

The word *analagous* describes something that is like something else. We can say, for example, that a clock or watch is a device that is analagous to our perception of the sun's movement across the sky. And we can think of other devices that are analagous to other things we find in nature. A thermometer is an "analog" device because the movement of the mercury in the tube or the pointer on a dial mimics the rise and fall of the temperature. Bathroom scales, barometers, and speedometers are other analog devices. We might say they are computers that compute by imitating the thing they measure.

During World War II, scientists and engineers learned how to build devices that could imitate the motion of aircraft. If a designer had an idea for a new kind of airplane, instead of building the actual plane he could build just an electronic model of it. Then by measuring the currents and voltages in the model, he could predict the probable characteristics and behavior of the plane itself without having to build it. The scientists and engineers also learned how to build electronic models of the flight of missiles and the movements of submarines and torpedoes, and almost anything else they could imagine.

All of these devices that imitate nature are called *analog computers*. Most things in nature change smoothly and continuously. The mercury in a thermometer does not jump from one position to the next, but moves up and down continuously along the thermometer scale. Similarly, a speedometer pointer moves continuously across the face of the speedometer. This kind of movement is a characteristic of analog computers; their "output" is always smooth and continuous.

An analog computer is a very satisfactory measuring device so long as it is to be used for just one purpose. But its limitations become obvious the moment we wish to use it for several different things. If we wish to change our electronic analog computer from, say a model of an aircraft to a model of a tank, we have to change the wiring inside the computer. This takes a long time, and is very tedious and probably expensive if we have to pay someone to do it.

An ordinary watch is a good example of an analog device dedicated to a single purpose—telling time. But many of today's electronic watches do much more than just tell time. They may monitor a person's pulse rate, act as a miniature calculator, and store a number of frequently called phone numbers. Some play a tune or have provisions for playing games on them. It would be almost impossible for an analog computer to be this *versatile,* and still be small enough to fit into a watch case.

So how is it done? Well, these new, multipurpose watches have a different kind of computer inside—a *digital* computer. Instead of mimicking something in nature like an analog computer, the digital computer uses just numbers—or digits—to do its computing. Analog computers are "measuring" computers, whereas digital computers are "counting" computers. This means that their "output" is not continuous but *discontinuous,* in contrast to the output of an analog computer. This may seem like a disadvantage of digital computers; but their output, for all practical purposes, can be made as smooth as we like.

The idea of computing by counting is very powerful because numbers are abstract. We can think of the number 4 in the context of 4 apples, 4 dollars, 4 votes—4 almost anything. And this is why digital computers are so much more versatile than analog computers; the numbers manipulated by the machine can represent whatever we wish, and we don't have to open up the digital computer and change its insides to make it do different things. All we have to do is give it a set of instructions—a *program* as it is called—that tells it what we want it to do. And these instructions, as we shall see more clearly later, are really nothing but patterns of numbers.

Throughout recorded history, people have developed devices to ease the tediousness of manipulating numbers. We wouldn't call these devices computers by today's standards, but they were milestones along the path that led to computers. One such device, developed at least two thousand five hundred years ago and still used widely today in certain parts of the world, is the *abacus.* Although there are different forms of this tool, the principle is basically the same in all— a system of beads strung on wires in a frame, in such a way that the beads can be moved back and forth as the computing progresses. A skilled abacus operator can keep up with or ahead of any calculating machine today, except an electronic computer.

Centuries after the abacus was developed, a young French mathematical genius, Blaise Pascal, invented the first real calculating machine, a small mechanical device with wheels that could add and subtract. Quite possibly he made his ma-

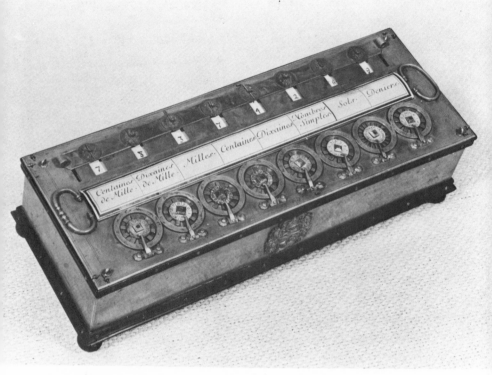

Pascal's calculating machine used wheels to add and subtract.

chine to help his tax-collector father, who, even in 1642, was overwhelmed by the burden of calculating returns.

A few years later a German mathematician improved Pascal's device so that it could do multiplication and division. During the 1700s many efforts were made to create a machine that could be produced commercially, but none were ever mass produced because of the difficulty of making multiple parts that would function properly. These mechanical calculators were products of their day at the beginning of the machine age with its cogs and wheels and levers. But it takes more than cogs and wheels to make a computer. What was needed was an entirely new idea, a new way of thinking about computing.

2.
Weaving Numbers

The cowcatcher on the front of a locomotive. The speedometer. The outrageous suggestion of charging a flat rate for all letters, no matter how far they travel. What have three such unrelated ideas in common? All were first conceived in the fertile mind of one man—Charles Babbage, born in Devonshire, England, in 1792. But what we most remember Babbage for is his "Analytical Engine," the father of all computers.

Babbage showed an early aptitude for mathematics and was one of the most ingenious thinkers of his time. When he entered Cambridge University in 1810, he knew more algebra than his tutor. While still at Cambridge, he and his friends started the "Analytical Society," whose ambitious purpose, according to its founders, was "to leave the world wiser than we found it."

Besides promoting his ideas for the cowcatcher and the speedometer, Babbage analyzed the pin-making industry, and later the operations of his own book publisher—who was so offended by Babbage's report that he refused to publish any more of Babbage's books. But the methods Babbage used were surprisingly close to what is today called "Operations Research."

Babbage's zeal for correcting errors wherever he found

*Charles Babbage was the
first to identify
the four basic parts
necessary to build
a computer.*

them and for improving everything on which his thought rested was not confined to mechanics. Having the soul of an accountant and not of a poet, he once took his distinguished fellow countryman Alfred Lord Tennyson to task for two lines Tennyson wrote in a long, solemn poem titled "The Vision of Sin":

> *Every moment dies a man,*
> *Every moment one is born.*

It must be manifest that if this were true, [Babbage wrote to Tennyson] the population of the world would be at a standstill. In truth the rate of birth is slightly in excess of that of death. I would suggest that in the next edition of your poem you have it read

> *Every moment dies a man,*
> *Every moment 1-1/16 is born.*

Strictly speaking this is not correct; the actual figure is so long that I cannot get it into a line, but I believe the figure 1-1/16 will be sufficiently accurate for poetry.

> *I am, Sir, yours, etc.*

Babbage was not the first to imagine the possibility of systematizing computations. At the end of the eighteenth century the French First Republic made an attempt to organize an "army" of mathematicians and dedicated workers to produce mathematical tables. The army was organized in the shape of a pyramid, with several mathematicians at the top who were to decide upon the best and most efficient computing methods. In the next level were a dozen or so competent workers who made calculations at selected points in the table. These were to serve as check points against which the final table could be compared. At the bottom of the pyramid were dozens of human computers who were to do the computations by rote, not deviating one "inch" from prescribed computational recipes. Although the approach was strictly nonmechanical, the system is comparable to modern computer techniques, in which the tasks performed are rigidly parceled out to the various parts of a computer.

Babbage's first attempt at building a calculating machine was inspired by his insatiable desire to correct errors he had detected in previously compiled tables, and to mechanize such tedious operations as calculating logarithm tables, which had been created many years before to ease the tasks of multiplying and dividing. To make the processes even easier, he devised his "Difference Engine," which was accurate to 6 decimal places. Later he tried to extend the accuracy to 20 decimal places. The British government was sufficiently interested in his project to contribute £17,000 toward its development. But the project was never completed because there were at that time no craftsmen who could build the necessary parts.

In 1833, Babbage gave up his Difference Engine in favor of his "Analytical Engine," which he continued working on until his death in 1871. The Difference Engine had been designed to perform only a limited number of operations,

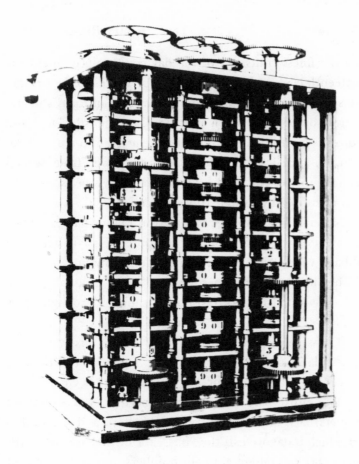

Babbage's Difference Engine was accurate to 6 decimal places.

but the Analytical Engine he planned to perform almost any conceivable mathematical operation.

Babbage devoted practically his entire fortune to his Analytical Engine. At one point he spent a good deal of time trying to work out a foolproof system for betting on horses to provide money for developing his machine. The attempt failed, of course, and no working model of the Analytical Engine was ever built during his lifetime.

The machine required thousands of parts that would work together with the greatest precision—a precision not even the finest craftsmen of the day could approach. In the nineteenth century, the parts had to be made from gears and levers and other available materials, instead of today's micro-electric components. Even if it had been possible to build Babbage's machine, it would not have fitted into ten railroad box cars, and it would have required power from several steam engines to run it—a far cry from today's pea-sized computer energized by a single tiny solar cell.

Nevertheless, Babbage's Analytical Engine had four parts that are today standard in any computer. First it had what Babbage called the "store." In modern computers we call this the "memory," or sometimes the "store," as Babbage did. Babbage wanted his store to hold a thousand 50-digit numbers.

The second part he called the "mill"; this was where the calculations would be performed. Today we call the mill the "central processing unit," or commonly, the "CPU."

The third part of Babbage's machine was to shuttle numbers back and forth between the store and the mill, a part which today we call the "bus," for obvious reasons. The fourth part was designed to get numbers into and out of the machine. In modern computers this is called "input-output." Later we shall say much more about these four parts of a computer.

In spite of his personal, financial, and mechanical problems, Babbage was not without supporters. His most unlikely ally was Augusta Ada, Countess of Lovelace—Lord Byron's only daughter. Like Babbage, Lady Lovelace showed an early aptitude for mathematics, and as a small child was taken to see Babbage's Difference Engine. Although she was the only child among the group of adults admiring the machine, she was, according to a later statement from one of the group, the only one "to understand the great beauty of the invention."

Punched paper cards instructed the Jacquard loom.

As an adult, Lady Lovelace wrote a technical account of the Analytical Engine that today is considered the most accurate source available. In it she said, "We may say most aptly that the Analytical Engine weaves algebraic patterns just as the Jacquard loom weaves flowers and leaves." In honor of Lady Lovelace's early recognition of Babbage's work, there is today a well-known language for programming computers called "ADA."

Lady Lovelace's mention of "the Jacquard loom" referred to the "store" in Babbage's Analytical Engine, the idea for which he had borrowed from a French silk weaver, Joseph Marie Jacquard. In 1800, Jacquard was asked to reconstruct an automated silk loom that had been built some sixty years earlier but was never used because the silk weavers of Lyons, France, were afraid the machine would put them out of work. As Jacquard reconstructed the machine, he made a few changes. The one that was crucial for the later development of the computer was the adoption of a punched paper card that "instructed" the loom which pattern to weave. Different cards contained instructions for different patterns, so that the weaver could change the pattern simply by replacing one card with another.

The idea of using paper with punched holes to control machines soon spread; by 1847, the principle was applied to a riveting machine used to build an iron bridge in Wales, and then later for building iron ships. These same ships were bringing immigrants to America by the thousands; and because of this influx of new people, it took nearly eight years to compile the results of the 1880 census count in the United States. By this time the information was so out of date that it was almost useless; and it was clear that with the ever-growing population, the 1890 census data would not be fully analyzed before 1900, when it would be time to take the *next* count. Something had to be done.

About this time a young engineer named Herman Hollerith was assigned to the surgeon general's office, which was responsible for the health statistics division of the census. Hollerith persuaded the Census Bureau to give him the contract for the 1890 census. His plan was to use "Jacquard's cards," about the size of a dollar bill, to store the data about people's age, sex, nationality, family size, occupation, and so on. The holes in the cards were punched in patterns that related to the kind of data stored. Hollerith also developed a machine that could sense the pattern of the holes automatically, so that enormous amounts of information could be quickly tabulated and analyzed. Using this system he was able to process the census data within two years after it was collected, a big improvement over the previous count.

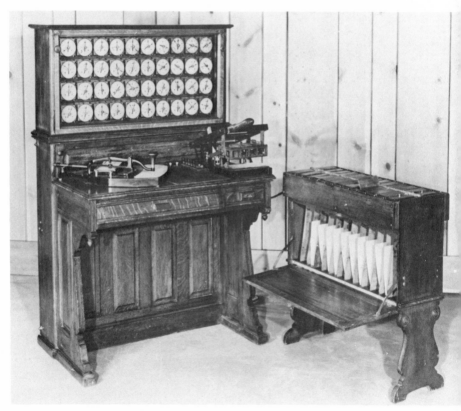

Hollerith's census tabulating machine enabled him to process the 1890 census data in two years.

Hollerith realized that his machines were useful for more than just handling the census. Soon the Hollerith cards—as they are still known today—were widely used in a variety of office machines. In 1896, Hollerith founded the Tabulating Machine Company, which later merged with three other companies to become the Computing-Tabulating-Recording Company. In 1911, it was renamed the International Business Machine Corporation (IBM). Hollerith's early machines were not what we would today call computers, but they did establish the great advantages of handling information with machines.

3.
From Brass Brains
to Silicon Cells

In 1900, off the Greek island of Antikythera, sponge divers made a remarkable discovery. On the bottom of the sea they found a corroded bronze box housing a complex mechanism of bronze gears. The exterior of the box was engraved with scales, and it had a pointer that was still intact. Instructions, inscribed in Greek, explained how to use the device. This first century analog computer apparently mimicked the motion of the planets, the sun, and the stars. But because the computer cogs and wheels could outrace the natural tracks of these heavenly bodies, it could predict their future movements.

Although this book is mainly about digital computers, it would be misleading not to say a little more about the important role of analog computers in the history of computing machines. Actually they made a more important and practical impact on mankind in the early years of this century than did the digital computer, even though Babbage had already mapped out most of the important elements of the digital computer.

The tides, like the sun and stars, are complex but reliable natural phenomena; and in 1905, the United States

Coast Guard sponsored the design of an 11-foot-long, 7-foot-high, 2,500-pound analog computer to foretell the tides. They called this computer, finished in 1910, the "Great Brass Brain." Each of its 37 dials—one for each variable in the prediction model—had to be set. Then an operator had to turn a crank, for as long as he had the strength, to predict the tides. Or he could turn the crank backward to recapture "lost" tides. After working faithfully for fifty-six years, the Great Brass Brain was retired in 1966.

Analog computers also played an important role in World War II. Over a decade before the beginning of the war, Dr. Vannever Bush and his associates at the Massachusetts Institute of Technology began work on a large analog computer that would later prove useful in determining the speed and trajectories of large-caliber bullets. The machine proved so useful, in fact, that a rumor was deliberately circulated saying that the computer project had failed, while all the time it was cranking out important results at a rate equal to the input of a hundred human operators using conventional desk calculators. But in spite of these early successes, the analog computer eventually gave way to the greater speed and versatility of the digital computer.

In the 1930s, digital computer technology was being developed in several places. In Germany a young engineer, Konrad Zuse, worked on a computer in his parents' living room. The descendants of this computer were later used to calculate wing designs for German aircraft.

In the United Kingdom the British, using the ideas of the brilliant English mathematician Alan Turing, developed a computer that led to the breaking of the German military codes.

In the United States, a few miles from the laboratory where Bush had worked on his analog computer, a young Harvard graduate student, Howard Aiken, was getting fed

The Mark I was built with electro-mechanical parts.

up with the tedious calculations required for his Ph.D. dissertation. So he designed and constructed a number of small, very specialized digital computers to make his work easier.

After a while he began to notice that all of his computers had many elements in common; all seemed to contain a set of primary constituents. Although Aiken was not aware of the work done by Babbage decades before, he was exploring the same ground. Sometime later, when someone pointed out Babbage's early work to him, Aiken said he felt that Babbage had been speaking directly to him from the past. In 1939, Aiken, with support from IBM, started work on a larger digital computer. Placed in operation at Harvard in 1943, this computer was called the Mark I.

During this time work was also going on at the Bell Telephone Laboratories under George Stibitz, a mathematician. Stibitz was the first to carry out computations over a telephone line, thus pointing the way to what is now called "remote" data processing.

Although these computers all had the essential ingredients of digital computers, they were still relatively slow because they were constructed largely from rather cumbersome and sluggish electric switches that operated mechanically. The first real breakthrough in increased speed was achieved by replacing the mechanical switches with vacuum tubes, which were faster and more reliable than the mechanical switches because they had no moving parts. During World War II, at the Moore School of Engineering, in Pennsylvania, J. Presper Eckert and John W. Mauchley, backed by the United States Army, built the first vacuum-tube computer. They dubbed it ENIAC (Electronic Numerical Integrator and Calculator). It was not finished until 1946, too late for help with the war effort, but it set the stage for today's high-speed, all-electronic digital computers.

ENIAC, however, was not without problems. The part of the computer that stored the program was somewhat like an old-style telephone switchboard, in which the wires have to be moved manually from one location to another to make the desired phone connections. Similarly, to reprogram the computer for a different task it was necessary to rewire its "switchboard" for each new application. And because of the heat generated by the vacuum tubes, one of its 18,000 tubes failed every seven minutes.

A Hungarian mathematical genius, John von Neumann, saw the solution to the rewiring problem: instead of reprogramming the computer for each new job by changing its wiring, why not store the program, as digital instructions, in the machine's memory along with the data? With this solution it is not only relatively easy to change the program, but the computer itself can modify the instructions, since they are simply strings of numbers stored in its own memory. The first commercial machine to incorporate a program stored in the computer was Univac 1, delivered to the United States Census Bureau in 1951.

In 1947, three scientists at the Bell Laboratories set upon a course that led to abandonment of the vacuum tube and thus solved the reliability problem. They were working on a new kind of switch made from *transistors,* which was to revolutionize the computer industry. Not only was the tran-

ENIAC was the first computer built with vacuum tubes.

sistor more reliable and thousands of times faster than vacuum tubes; it was also cheaper and smaller, and it generated very little heat.

In a few years the scientists at the Bell Laboratories had produced the first all-transistorized computer, the Leprechaun. But fearful of antitrust action from the Justice Department, the Bell Labs decided to license others to build the transistor. Soon a number of new companies as well as old-line tube manufacturers were stamping out transistors.

In the early days of transistors, electronic devices were wired together with a maze of wires much as they had been with vacuum tubes. Anyone who has looked inside an old vacuum-tube radio will understand the problem; if repairs were needed, it was difficult to remove and replace the wires and defective parts. And building the radio in the first place was a tedious and largely manual task.

Then someone realized that the matchhead-size transistors could be connected by wires printed on boards. But that was only the beginning. In the late 1950s several scientists saw that the transistors, the wiring, and all could be etched directly onto a piece of silicon. These *integrated circuits,* or *chips,* are produced by the millions today, for just pennies each.

But there was even more to come. Chips, like the analog computer, had one serious drawback; etched in silicon they could not be altered, and so could perform only the function they were designed for. Then, in 1971, the Intel Corporation announced the "programmable" chip. Incredibly, one of these chips contained the entire central processing unit (CPU) of a computer. Today these programmable chips are called *microprocessors,* and they are at the heart of the computer revolution, spawning everything from TV video games to personal computers. The Babbage mill can now literally be fitted into the eye of a needle.

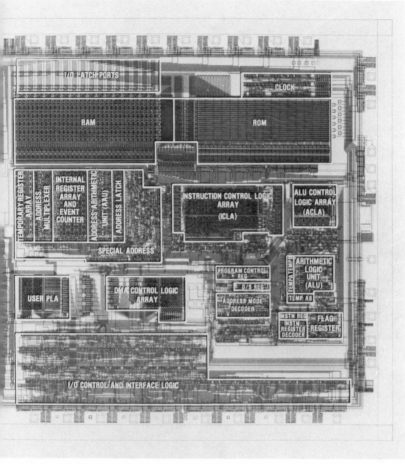

Magnified view of a computer chip.

The most visible changes in the development of the computer in this century have been from large, slow, noisy, unreliable, and energy-hungry computers to small, swift, quiet, reliable, diet-conscious computers. But these are really only changes in the sophistication of our technology and do not represent what we might call the fundamental aspects of computers. Next we shall look more deeply into what separates the computer, in such a profound way, from any other machine man has ever built.

4.
The Machine with a Million Faces

In the last two centuries man has expanded his limited physical powers in ways that would have seemed impossible—even magical—in the days before the industrial revolution. Machines let him pull loads that a thousand horses harnessed together could not budge, cruise beneath the sea, and fly to the moon.

If man can use machines to expand his physical powers, why not his mental powers also? Early calculating machines like the abacus extended man's arithmetic abilities. These were important steps, as were later, more sophisticated calculators such as the slide rule and the adding machine. But none of these machines, including the simple electronic calculators, even come close to what we today call a *computer*.

Why? Because a computer is *versatile*. A computer that could only solve certain mathematical equations or compute tax tables would be helpful but dull. A truly useful, "smart" computer would tackle almost any conceivable computational task, from counting beans or multiplying and dividing numbers to controlling a microwave oven and predicting the weather. Babbage understood this point very well; hence his lifelong effort to perfect his Analytical Engine.

But how could such a machine be built? One answer is to build a machine composed of many parts. Part 1 does task 1; part 2 does task 2; part 3 does task 3, and so on. But this is little more than a collection of many machines in one place; and as new tasks are assigned to such a machine, new parts must be added until the machine bogs down under its own weight.

Babbage's idea was to build a machine with parts that could be combined in different ways to perform different tasks—in the same way that bricks can be assembled in endless varieties to build anything from a simple bookcase to a majestic cathedral. The brick by itself is hardly anything at all—it's just a brick. But that characteristic is its great virtue. If the brick itself suggested any particular application, its versatility would be limited. Bricks in the shape of giant doughnuts, for example, stacked one on another, would be ideal for building chimneys, but they would hardly do for a garden path.

The trick with bricks, as with the parts of Babbage's computer, is to have a plan. And if the task is complex, whether it is a building or a computer problem, the ingenuity of the solution is largely up to the planner.

One of the early planners was Alan Turing, the English mathematician mentioned in the previous chapter, who led the attack on cracking the German military code during World War II. Turing, only a mediocre student in school, is a towering figure in the history of computers, and also one of the most eccentric.

As is often the case with creative geniuses, Turing never saw the world quite the way others did. His mother told a story about him that illustrates this characteristic. Turing owned a bicycle whose chain fell off at periodic intervals. He soon discovered that the chain always fell off after a certain number of revolutions of the pedals; so as he pedaled down the street he would count the revolutions and then jump off the bike at just the right moment and push the chain back on. Later, to avoid the burden of keeping track of the pedal revolutions, he fixed a device to the bicycle handlebars that automatically counted the revolutions. The problem with the bike could have been solved in a matter of minutes, since it was due to a bent spoke that, when it came in alignment with a faulty link in the chain, caused the chain to fall off. But to the whimsical Turing, such a solution would have been dull and uninteresting.

In the early part of World War II, Turing and a number of other outstanding mathematicians and electronic wizards were recruited by the British Government to investigate the science of code making and code breaking—cryptography. The first codes were created by hand, but eventually machines took over. One such German machine, the Enigma, fell into the hands of the Polish secret service and was shipped to England. The purpose of the Enigma was to scramble messages in such a way that they could be decoded only by another Enigma machine set according to the correct "key." We could think of the Enigma as a lock, and Turing and his colleagues had the job of finding the key that would unlock it.

Turing played a leading part in designing the computer that finally provided the key. Series of computers were produced during the war years, including one called the Colossus series. These computers were located in a country house in Hertfordshire, about fifty miles from London. As intercepted messages were decoded, they were sent directly to Britain's wartime prime minister, Winston Churchill. Some historians believe that the ability to decipher the secret German messages was decisive in the Allied victory.

But Turing's interest in computers was broader than simply cracking codes. Naturally curious, he wanted to know what computers could and could not do. Just as there are limits to what people can do with bricks, so there are limits to what machines, including computers, can do. The perpetual motion machine, for instance, has always been a dream of mankind; and even today there is an occasional news story of someone who claims to have invented such a machine. But we know that such claims are always false—not because of any detailed analysis of the purported machine, but because the very idea contradicts one of the basic laws of nature—the "Second Law of Thermodynamics."

This law emerged as scientists investigated the underlying principles governing all machines. What it means in simple terms is that "you can't get something for nothing." To do work we need energy, only part of which goes into the work we wish to do. A certain part of the energy is always wasted. As we shall see later, there are laws like the Second Law of Thermodynamics that restrict the ability of computers to make every conceivable computation.

It was matters of this kind that Turing wished to investigate. Babbage had believed that his Analytical Engine—had he ever been able to build it—could cope with almost any kind of mathematical problem; but he was never able to prove his idea to the satisfaction of mathematicians. This is just what Turing set out to do. He was interested in using computers to solve purely mathematical problems, and also in the possibility of building "intelligent" computers. We shall consider "intelligent" computers in our final chapter, but now we shall discuss what has come to be known as the "Universal Turing Machine."

In the early days of the industrial revolution, scientists tried to understand the basic characteristics of machines by studying ideal, abstract machines that had never been built, but existed only on paper. This is how they discovered the Second Law of Thermodynamics. In just such a way, Turing

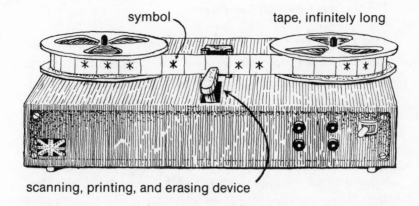

symbol

tape, infinitely long

scanning, printing, and erasing device

fig. 1   Turing Machine (artist's conception)

was studying the basic properties of computers that existed only on paper. He hoped to discover something like a Second Law of Thermodynamics for computers—a universal law, or laws, that applied to all computers, not just specific ones.

Turing's Universal Machine was a strange affair. Through it passed an infinitely long tape, like ticker tape, marked off in squares. Each square contained a symbol—perhaps a letter of the alphabet, or simply a 0 or a 1. The tape moved through the machine one square at a time, forward or backward. As the machine scanned the squares, inspecting each one, it could either remove a symbol or replace it with another. See Figure 1.

Such a machine seems good for hardly anything at all. But then, a person seeing a brick by itself might make a similar judgment; the shape of the brick suggests hardly anything. We have seen, however, that it is this very feature of the brick that is the secret of its great usefulness, and so it is with the Turing machine. Turing was able to show that his simple machine is capable of doing any calculation that any conceivable special-purpose computer could ever do. Or stated a little differently, if a computation can't be done with a Turing machine, it can't be done with any machine. So the

Turing machine represents a kind of universal computer that can be studied to reveal the characteristics and limitations of any existing or future computer.

Another important feature of the Turing machine can be illustrated by our analogy of the bricks. The fact that bricks are small contributes to their universal usefulness. If bricks were the size of bathtubs, we could never make a doghouse with them; one brick would be as big as the whole doghouse. Of course, if we were building the pyramids, bathtub-size bricks would be an advantage, since it would take fewer bricks to do the job. We see here what is called a "trade-off." With big bricks we can build pyramids faster, but we can't build doghouses.

Earlier we saw another kind of trade-off: with doughnut-shaped bricks we could build chimneys easily, but not garden paths. All of this suggests that the more specialized the brick, the easier it is to build a particular kind of structure—but only *that* structure. With more "abstract" bricks we can build a greater variety of structures, but the project always requires more bricks, time, and effort.

Turing's paper computer is the ultimate in abstract computers; that is why it is the *Universal* Turing Machine. But as we might expect, even the simplest operations with this machine are lengthy and seemingly complex. As an example, let's consider the simple operation of multiplying 2×3 with a Turing machine. First we need some rules to tell the machine whether to move the tape to the right or to the left, and whether to erase a mark on the tape or to print a mark. In our machine we shall use just two symbols—a blank space and an asterisk*. After the machine has inspected a square and either erased or printed an asterisk, the rules also need to tell the machines what to do next.

To do our multiplication problem, we will need to give the machine four rules:

1. Move the tape one square to the right and inspect the square. If it is blank, return to rule 1 and repeat it. If the square is not blank, erase the asterisk and go to rule 2.

2. Move the tape one square to the left and inspect the square. If it is blank, print an asterisk and go on to rule 3. If it is not blank, leave the asterisk and return to rule 2 and repeat it.

3. Move the tape one square to the left and inspect the square. If it is blank, print an asterisk and go to rule 4. If it is not blank, leave the asterisk and return to rule 3 and repeat it.

4. Move the tape one square to the right and inspect the square. If it is blank, leave it blank and return to rule 1. If it is not blank, leave the asterisk and return to rule 4 and repeat it.

On first reading, these rules seem arbitrary and abstract, with no relation at all to multiplying. But we might expect this to be the case with a universal machine using just two symbols.

Table 1 shows the "status" of the machine at each step it needs to multiply 2 × 3. To understand the table, think first of an endless tape marked off in squares, as shown in Fig. 2; the tape moves back and forth as the machine inspects one square at a time and prints an asterisk, erases an asterisk, or leaves the square as it is, according to the rule being applied at that step. The numbers of the squares in Figure 2 correspond to the column numbers in the table. Imagine each line of the table as the tape, marked off in squares, as in Figure 2.

Let's look now at step 1 of the table. In columns 11, 12, and 13 we see asterisks; these represent the number 3, which we wish to multiply by 2. The 2 is "built into" the four rules,

5	6	7	8	9	10	11	12	13	14	15	16	STEP	RULE
					↓	*	*	*				1	1
						↓	*	*				2	1
					↓*		*	*				3	2
				↓*		*	*	*				4	3
				*	↓*		*	*				5	4
				*	*	↓	*	*				6	4
				*	*		↓	*				7	1
				*	*	↓*		*				8	2
				*	↓*	*		*				9	3
				↓*	*	*		*				10	3
			↓*	*	*	*		*				11	3
			*	↓*	*	*		*				12	4
			*	*	↓*	*		*				13	4
			*	*	*	↓*		*				14	4
			*	*	*	*	↓	*				15	4
			*	*	*	*		↓				16	1
			*	*	*	*	↓*					17	2
			*	*	*	↓*	*					18	3
			*	*	↓*	*	*					19	3
			*	↓*	*	*	*					20	3
			↓*	*	*	*	*					21	3
		↓*	*	*	*	*	*					22	4
		*	↓*	*	*	*	*					23	4
		*	*	↓*	*	*	*					24	4
		*	*	*	↓*	*	*					25	4
		*	*	*	*	↓*	*					26	4
		*	*	*	*	*	↓*					27	4
		*	*	*	*	*	*	↓				28	4
		*	*	*	*	*	*		↓			29	1
		*	*	*	*	*	*			↓		30	1

Table 1

which are the steps of a "doubling program." They could be used to double—or multiply by 2—any number, simply by starting out with the number of asterisks on the tape in step 1 that we wish to multiply by 2. We shall discuss the rules in a little more detail as soon as we complete our simple problem of multiplying 2 × 3; doing this exercise will help us to visualize what the machine is doing and how the rules work.

The arrow in each line shows which square the machine is inspecting at that step; in line 1, the arrow means that the machine is inspecting square 10. Since it is blank, the machine should, according to rule 1, move on to the next square

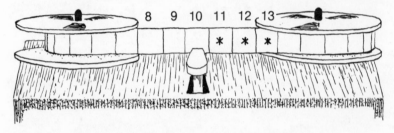

step 1.   Machine inspects square 10, which is blank. The three asterisks represent the number 3, which we wish to multiply by 2.

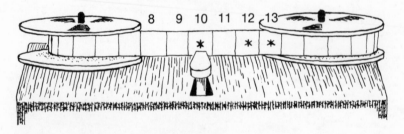

step 3.   Machine again inspects square 10 and prints an asterisk.
In step 2 it erased the asterisk in square 11.

fig. 2

to the right—square 11—and apply rule 1 again. This is step 2. Now the machine "sees" an asterisk, and according to rule 1, it should erase the asterisk and move on to rule 2.

We are now ready for step 3. Rule 2 says to move one square to the left and inspect the square. We see that this rule has been carried out because in step 3 the arrow has moved to the left from square 11 to square 10. We also see that an asterisk has been printed in square 10, as it should have been, according to rule 2, since square 10 was originally blank.

We shall not go through all of the steps here, but anyone who is interested can follow the table step by step and prove to himself that the machine always obeys the rules, one step at a time.

Let's look at step 27. Here we see asterisks in columns 7, 8, 9, 10, 11, and 12—six asterisks in all, which is the answer to our problem: $2 \times 3 = 6$: We have also included a few steps beyond 27 to show that, since all the rest of the squares on the tape are blank, the machine is forever "stuck" in rule 1. This is because rule 1 says to move to the right and if the square is blank to return to rule 1 and move to the right—over and over again. A better computer *program*—our four rules are an example of a computer program because they tell the computer what to do—would shut the machine off after the answer was first obtained, at step 22.

The rules in our program are rather hard to grasp because we can't hold all of the details in mind at once. But as we look at the table we see that it starts out with 3 asterisks, and at step 22 it ends up with 6 asterisks—the answer to 2×3.

If we look at the zigzag pattern of the arrows in the table, we can see "what is going on." First the computer searches squares to the right until it finds an asterisk, which it erases. This erased asterisk—now a blank space—serves as a "marker" later on. Then the computer searches to the *left* until it finds a blank space, which it replaces with an asterisk. We are now at step 4. Next the computer searches again to the right until it finds a blank space, which it replaces with an asterisk two steps later in step 8. The blank space it finds at this point is the one it left as a "marker" in a previous step. By moving back and forth and leaving markers, the program systematically duplicates—or doubles—the 3 original asterisks, so that we eventually end up with 6 asterisks.

If we had started out with 5 asterisks, we would have ended up with 10. This is so because, as we have said this particular set of four rules is a doubling program. We could write other sets of rules for a tripling program, a "quintupling" program, and so on; and in this way we could build up a number of programs to do whatever arithmetic we wish.

Looking at the rules themselves, we see that each one has just two alternatives: if the square is blank, do this; if it has an asterisk, do that. This fact brings up an important point. Most machines have their own way of doing things. Computers like doing calculations with just two symbols—usually 0's and 1's—or *binary* arithmetic, as it is called. People like doing arithmetic in the decimal system, which probably stems from primitive counting systems based on the ten fingers. Babbage's Analytical Engine was based on the decimal system, using the digits 0 through 9.

A contemporary of Babbage's, George Boole, developed a system of algebra that dealt with just 0's and 1's. Boole, of course, didn't know it at the time, but as happens so often in science, he was developing exactly the kind of algebra that computer theorists needed to gain a truly deep understanding of the inner workings and limitations of computers.

Still, because we like to work in the decimal system, it is difficult for us to program computers in their own binary language. We would like to be able to talk to the computer in a language that is closer to our own. In Chapter 6 we shall have more to say about programming languages that are closer to human language and much easier to understand than the four rules we gave our Turing machine to multiply 2×3, which are in the language of the machine. Today most computers are programmed in these more natural "high-level" languages, and then the computer itself translates the high-level language into its own binary language.

Turing was able to prove with his paper machine that it would be possible to construct an all-purpose computer that could be programmed to solve any problem that any special-purpose computer could solve. He was also able to show that there are some problems that computers cannot solve. Later we shall discuss some problems that computers will never be able to solve. But before we do that, we shall learn about an invention that turned Turing's paper machines into real machines.

5.
A Thousand Computers in a Thimble

What are "bigger" when they are smaller, cheaper by the dozen, and even cheaper by the million? Computers. Incredibly perhaps, future grapefruit-size computers will be thousands of times more powerful than today's computers.

The road to miniaturization began in 1947 with the invention of the transistor. The transistor, a hundred times smaller than the vacuum tube which it replaced, looked like a pea with three short wires for legs; and it could be powered by a tiny battery. If we compare the first vacuum-tube computer, the 20-ton ENIAC, with today's microcomputer, we find that the ENIAC had 100,000 electrical components filling a two-car garage, whereas the microcomputer, with one million electrical components, rests on an area smaller than a postage stamp.

The microcomputer can be powered by less energy than it takes to run a nightlight; its ENIAC ancestor required more than thirty thousand times as much energy. And the microcomputer can do a million calculations per second, compared to ENIAC's one-hundred thousand.

But as we saw in our discussion of Turing machines, even the simplest problem done in binary arithmetic requires

The vacuum tube, the base of which appears on the left, was replaced by the pea-size transistor, which was reduced in size so that thousands could be packed onto a single chip.

a multitude of steps; so the transistor was just what was needed to turn computers into a practical reality, not just for well-heeled banks and large industries, but for everybody.

The first transistor was only the first step in miniaturization. We have learned that whole computers now reside on flakes of silicon. How has this mindboggling achievement come about? If you were to enter one of today's modern transistor factories, you might imagine that you were in a large hospital operating room, with people scurrying here and there in antiseptic white gowns while others peer into microscopes. Every precaution is taken to make sure that only authorized personnel enter the "clean rooms," and even they must enter through specially constructed doors that keep out unwanted dust and other contaminants. For a tiny transistor nestled with thousands of others on a chip, a speck of dust would be as damaging as a rock in an egg-sorting machine.

The first step in making a chip starts with a rod of almost pure crystalline silicon, perhaps 3 to 5 inches in diameter. These rods, somewhat like rock candy, are "grown" under the most careful conditions so that their crystalline structure is as nearly perfect as man knows how to make it.

Next the rods are sliced into wafers as thin as a razor blade; these are baked in ovens, like cookies on a cookie sheet, at temperatures near 2000 degrees Fahrenheit. The air in the ovens is rich with oxygen, so that the silicon wafers become coated or "rusted" with a thin layer of silicon dioxide.

After they are taken from the oven, the wafers are coated with an emulsion similar to the coating on photographic film called a photoresist. The photoresist is sensitive to ultraviolet light, which is at frequencies too high for the human eye to detect. Ultraviolet light is used because its wavelength is shorter—and so has a higher frequency—than ordinary light. At these short wavelengths, the circuits on the silicon chip can be etched more precisely and delicately than is possible with ordinary light.

The next step is to cover the wafer with a template or mask that covers up parts of the wafer and leaves other parts uncovered. When the wafer is exposed to ultraviolet light, the photoresist on the parts of the wafer that are not covered becomes "hardened." Then when the wafer is dipped in an acid bath—the next step—the unexposed parts wash away, down to the original silicon surface, leaving just the hardened parts.

At this point, if we looked at a wafer under a microscope we would see a complex landscape with the valleys corresponding to the parts of the wafer etched away by the acid bath, and the ridges and hills the hardened parts that have withstood the acid bath, as shown in the bottom drawing of Figure 1. The chip landscape, of course, is dictated by the shape of the mask.

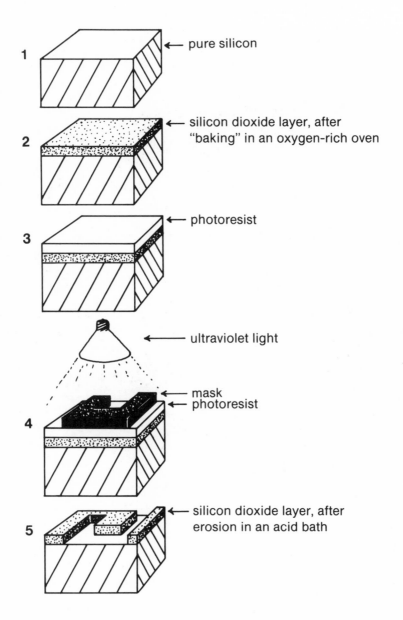

1 ← pure silicon

2 ← silicon dioxide layer, after "baking" in an oxygen-rich oven

3 ← photoresist

← ultraviolet light

← mask
← photoresist

4

5 ← silicon dioxide layer, after erosion in an acid bath

fig. 1   Making a chip—a cross section of part of a wafer

Designing and making the mask is one of the most diffi-cult parts of making a chip, for it is a map of the electronic components and connecting circuits that make up the chip.

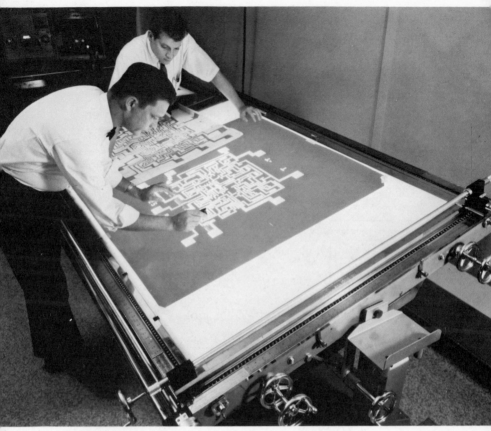

Preparing the mask to be used in making a chip.

The map is first laid out on paper at a scale with which human eyes and hands can cope. At this stage such a map might cover an entire gymnasium floor if fully spread out. The complexity of the map could easily exceed that of a map of New York City with all its streets and avenues, alleys, and side streets.

After everyone is satisfied that the "map" represents all of the circuits correctly, it is photographically reduced—somewhat like looking through a telescope backwards, so that everything is made much smaller—until it will fit many times over on a single wafer. This gives the wafer a checker-board

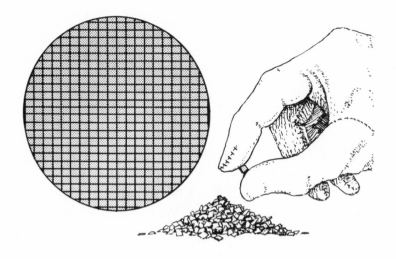

fig. 2   Slice of silicon rod cut into chips

appearance, and inside of each square is an exact duplicate of the original map, with all the valleys and ridges. Thus a single wafer can be cut up, like a round pan full of fudge, to produce many duplicates of the same chip, as shown in Figure 2.

But this is only part of the process. Like New York City, a chip is not all on one level. It has its underground subways, its overhead highways, and its many-storied buildings. In fact, a single chip may have as many as a dozen interconnected levels, each with its own detailed map plus maps showing how all the levels are connected with one another.

A magnified view of part of a chip, showing its many layers.

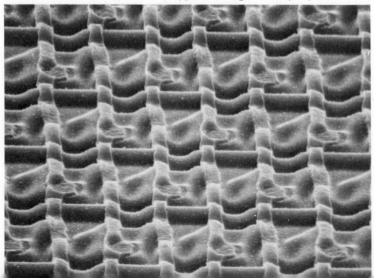

In the most advanced chips this amount of detail is too much for the human mind to handle, so computers are now routinely used to help design new chips. The stage is rapidly reached where chips are being designed by computers whose chips were designed by other computers, resulting in computers so complex that no human being can possibly know the details of any advanced computer.

American Nobel Prize-winning physicist Richard P. Feynman once commented, "There is always room at the bottom"—a parody of the familiar saying that "There is always room at the top." What Feynman had in mind was that we could build a machine that would make smaller versions of itself, which would in turn make even smaller versions of itself, and so on—always finding "more room at the bottom." This is not as crazy as it sounds. Later we shall discuss the possibility of building electrical components from individual molecules, so that we could put into a domino more electrical components than have been built in the entire world to date.

We've described the process for making chips from thousands of transistors, but we haven't said much about how transistors calculate. As impossible as it may seem, all computer operations can be carried out by using just a few simple devices built from transistors. Two of these devices are called "AND gates" and "OR gates."

Let's consider an AND gate first. Figure 3 shows a device made from a transistor that has two wires going into it and one coming out. We have labeled the ingoing wires "A" and "B," and the outgoing wire "C." The device works in a simple way: if two electrical signals are traveling along the wires A and B at the same time, then the device lets a signal pass out through wire C. This is why the device is called an AND gate; the gate opens to let something out at C only if something is present simultaneously at A *and* B.

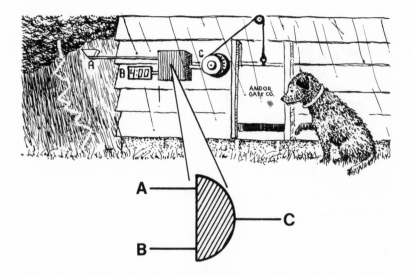

fig. 3   This device is an AND gate if it emits a signal at C when signals are present on A *and* B.
It is an OR gate if it emits a signal at C when signals are present on either A *or* B.

At this point the electrical signals are just "electrical signals"; so we may let them represent anything we wish. The A signal may represent rain, and the B signal the time of day—say 4:00 in the afternoon. And the C signal, when it is present, might activate a motor that opens a door. We might use this device thus: if it is raining—creating an A signal, *and* if it is after 4:00 in the afternoon—creating a B signal, then C will be present to open a door that lets the family dog in from the back yard.

Some people might object that this is not a nice way to treat a family pet. Shouldn't the dog be let in *whenever* it is raining? A device essentially the same in structure but "wired" differently is an OR gate, which works like this: If it is raining—creating an A signal, *or* if it is after 4:00 in the afternoon—creating a B signal, then C will be present if either A *or* B is present.

In this particular application, the AND and OR gates act as "logical" devices because they represent the idea that if A is true and B is true, then C is true; or if A or B is true, then C is true. Later we shall have much more to say about computers as "logical" devices.

Now let's consider using an AND gate for doing arithmetic. We'll take the simple problem of adding 1 to 1. As before, we can let the signals A, B, and C represent anything we wish. Here we shall let signal A represent the number 1; and similarly, B will represent a 1. C will represent a 2. If we wish to add $1 + 1$, then both signals A and B will be present, producing signal C, or 2.

This simple adder is a long way from doing complex arithmetic, but arrays of such devices hooked together in the proper way can add, substract, multiply, and divide any numbers we like. In fact, multiplying is simply the same thing as adding the same number to itself the desired number of times. The problem 2×3 is the same as 2 added to itself three times $(2 \times 3 = 2 + 2 + 2)$. This is the way computers multiply; they just add the number to itself the correct number of times, but they do it so fast that we imagine that the process is more mysterious than it is. And since dividing is just the inverse of multiplying, computers divide by subtracting in a similar way.

Because of the strict logical nature of the devices that go into computers, computers are very exacting. An AND gate, if it is working properly, would never operate on a "maybe" basis—if A and B are true, well, then, *maybe* C. Only people operate that way: If I get home from school by 4:00, and if it is raining, well, then maybe I'll let the dog in—if I'm not eating a peanut butter sandwich, and if my friend isn't talking to me on the phone.

One of the reasons computers are so hard to program is that they are so completely exact, or "logical," as computer scientists say; they do exactly what we tell them to do, even if what we tell them to do is dumb. Very often we give them dumb instructions, not realizing that they are dumb. Our minds aren't rigid, logical machines; so more often than not we make hazy, ambiguous statements which, when translated into a program, leave the computer confused and sometimes marching off in the wrong direction. Or it may move in the right direction for a time and then start running in circles. You may recall that our program to multiply 2×3, using the Turing machine, left the machine in a state of running on forever—not a very good practice, considering the high costs of computer time.

It appears that the "gates" in the human mind do not operate on a strictly all-or-nothing basis. A typical gate—or neuron, as it is called in the brain—might have fifty thousand input signals, instead of just two. And if we required that fifty thousand things be true at the same time before some action was taken, it seems likely that nothing would ever be done. Human gates seem to operate on the "almost" principle. But it is this very feature that allows human beings to take action with incomplete information. This whole subject of the similarity between computers and the human mind is very controversial, and we shall consider it more fully in the final chapter of this book.

We have seen that talking to a computer is not easy. Computers insist on precise, step-by-step instructions, and their language is limited to 0's and 1's—no's and yes's, with no in-between positions. Let's look now at some attempts that have been made to make talking to computers easier.

6.
Talking to Computers

"Why did you do that?" she gasped, staring at the close-cropped, red-orange ringlets on her image in the mirror.

"Because you said that's what you wanted," he answered calmly.

"But you know that's not what I wanted, even if it is what I said," she protested.

We've all heard or taken part in conversations like this, and we've all been startled—and sometimes amused—because someone responded literally to something we expressed vaguely, incompletely, or without thinking it through carefully.

We may become irritated or puzzled because a computer does just what we tell it to do, but we really can't complain or argue. As we know by now, computers are logical and literal; they do exactly what we tell them to do. So quite often we find that what we thought we had told the computer to do is not, in fact, what we asked for. Marvelous as their feats are, computers are a long way from responding to the subtleties of human expression and meaning. We cannot expect them to read our mind and interpret our thoughts. So talking to computers is quite different from talking to people.

There are similarities, however. When people communicate with each other, they need basically four things: First they need something to communicate; this may be just the cry of a baby that says, "I'm hungry." Or it may be a vast "store" of information—facts and ideas accumulated in a human being's "memory." Second, people need the ability to think—to combine facts and ideas stored in memory to arrive at new ideas and conclusions. These two functions are generally thought of as functions of the brain.

The other two needs are for "input" and "output"— some way to get information into and out of the brain. The physical senses—sight, hearing, taste, smell, and touch—are all "sensors" through which we take in information. And our abilities to speak, sing, write, draw, make gestures, and so on provide avenues for getting information out of the brain and "displaying" it for others.

As we know from our discussion of Babbage's Analytical Engine, all computers also have these four basic components. The store or memory and the "mill" that processes material in the memory comprise the computer itself—the "brain." The input may be a signal from a sensor that "feels" temperature or humidity, or it may be a circuit hooked to a "data base" hundreds of miles away. Commonly it is a signal from a keyboard much like a typewriter keyboard, on which anyone wishing to talk to the computer types out instructions or questions. The output may be a signal from a device that turns on an air-conditioning system or controls a microwave oven. Commonly a computer displays its output on a cathode ray tube (CRT), which is much like an ordinary TV screen. Or it may be hooked up to a printer that makes a more permanent record of what it "says."

Another essential for communication, of course, is a language that all concerned can understand. As we saw earlier, the Turing machine required quite explicit instructions to carry out the simple task of multiplying 2×3. The binary language is so foreign to human modes of thinking that it wasn't at all clear to us what the instructions given to the machine had to do with multiplying. What we need to talk to a computer is a system that combines the precision of statement demanded by the computer with a way of expressing commands in a more natural language.

Computer scientists call the language of a computer "machine language"; our instructions for the Turing machine were in machine language. The first small step toward a more natural kind of language was called "assembly language." In assembly language some of the machine language instructions, which are all in 0's and 1's, are replaced by words that make it easier to write programs.

But before the computer can get to work, it must have the instructions in machine language. So we give the computer another task—to translate the assembly language into machine language. It does this by using a program called an "assembler." This process is another example of the versatility of computers—the machine becomes its own interpreter.

Still assembly language is not easy to use because most programs contain many hundreds and even thousands of commands. The programmer must understand the computer's peculiar capacities and limitations in responding to commands. He or she must make sure that the commands are not redundant—that is, that the same commands are not included in a different part of the program; that sufficient memory is reserved in the computer for intermediate results—a kind of "computer scratch pad"; that the commands can be executed in a way that achieves the maximum speed of operation; and that many other what we might call "housekeeping chores" are taken care of.

In 1954, work was started on a new kind of programming language called a "high level" language. To get a sense of a high-level language, let's consider the simple, specific command, "Sit down." Obeying this command involves several steps: Find a vacant chair. Position yourself in front of it. Bend your knees until your posterior settles on the chair. All these steps are at the level of machine language, whereas the command "sit down" is at the level of a high-level language. Languages like BASIC, COBOL, and FORTRAN are high-level languages, closer to natural language than is assembly language; and they also took care of many of the housekeeping details. But they are still far from natural language.

One of the most popular high-level languages is BASIC, which stands for Beginner's All-purpose Symbolic Instruction Code. After a few hours of training and practice, almost anyone can write a simple program in BASIC. Such a program consists of a number of commands or statements whose order of execution is determined by numbering each statement so that the computer begins with the lowest numbered statement and proceeds to the next until all commands have been carried out.

Let's write a simple program in BASIC to determine the distance a car moves in a certain length of time as it travels along a highway at a constant speed. We know, for example, that a car going thirty miles per hour will have moved fifteen miles after one half hour. In other words, the distance a car moves is equal to the speed multiplied by the time the car travels. To save time, instead of writing out distance, speed, and time each time we wish to use these ideas, we'll just write D for distance, S for speed, and T for time. So our recipe or formula for determining distance is distance equals speed multiplied by time, or $D = S * T$. (Computer programmers usually use the symbol "$*$" for multiplying rather than the letter "x" to avoid confusion.)

We wish to write our program so that it can compute the distance for any speed or length of time—not just one specific speed or length of time. So we shall write the program in such a way that the computer first asks us what length of time we are interested in, and then asks us what speed we wish to use. These two steps, or statements, in our program look like this:

> 1   INPUT T
> 2   INPUT S

When we "run" this program on our computer, the first thing it does is to go to step 1, the lowest numbered step, which means, in BASIC, "Type on the keyboard the desired length of time, T." How does the computer tell us to do this? Well, in this particular program, a question mark (?) would appear on the screen, meaning that the computer is waiting for us to type in a length of time—say 2 hours.

After we type in a 2, for 2 hours, the computer moves on to step 2; and now another question mark appears, meaning that the computer is waiting for us to type a speed. Let's type in 10, meaning the speed is 10 miles per hour.

At this point the computer knows—has stored in its memory—that the travel time we are interested in is 2 hours and the speed is 10 miles per hour. Now it would search for the next step—which we haven't written yet. So for the next step, step 3, we instruct the computer to compute the distance traveled by the car in 2 hours at 10 miles per hour. Step 3 is $D = S$ T.

Our program so far is

> 1   INPUT T
> 2   INPUT S
> 3 $D = S * T$

Step 3 practically explains itself. It means to the computer, multiply S times T and call the answer D. The computer already knows that T is 2 hours and S is 10 miles per hour; so in step 3 it sets D equal to 20 miles (2 hours times 10 miles per hour equals 20 miles). The computer then stores the value of D—20 miles—in its memory.

Now the computer knows the answer, but *we* still do not know it. We need to tell the computer to show us the answer. So in step 4 we command it to do this. In BASIC, step 4 looks like this: PRINT D.

Now the program looks like this:

$$1 \quad \text{INPUT} \quad \text{T}$$
$$2 \quad \text{INPUT} \quad \text{S}$$
$$3 \quad \text{D} = \text{S} * \text{T}$$
$$4 \quad \text{PRINT} \quad \text{D}$$

Statement 4 in BASIC tells the computer to print, or display, the answer, which is 20, on the screen. So at the end of step 4 we would see a "20" there.

After it has completed step 4, the computer looks for the next step. But our program has accomplished its task, so in step 5 we tell the computer that the program is over. Step 5 simply says, END.

Suppose we wished to determine the distances a number of different cars traveling at different speeds and for differing lengths of time have traveled. Car 1 might have moved at 12 miles per hour for 1 hour; car 2, 47 miles per hour for 7 hours; car 3, 39 miles per hour for 3 hours; and so on. We could rerun our program over and over, one time for each car. Or we could rewrite the program in such a way that as soon as the computer had printed out the value of the distance on the screen, it would automatically start over, each time waiting for us to type in new values for time and speed. This is an easy thing to do in BASIC. We simply replace the

END command in statement 5 with a GOTO command, so that our program looks like this:

```
1  INPUT T
2  INPUT S
3  D = S * T
4  PRINT D
5  GOTO 1
```

In BASIC, statement 5 tells the computer to return to statement 1 and start the program all over. Statement 1, of course, causes a question mark to appear on the screen, meaning we should enter a value for T before the computer proceeds to step 2; and when it again reaches step 5, this step tells the computer to start again at step 1.

This kind of program is "circular" because it keeps going around and around as long as we keep entering new values for T and S. These circular paths, or "loops" as they are called, are very powerful programming tools because they allow a computer to repeat the same operation over and over without our having to write out the directions each time.

But the loops are also responsible for some of the biggest problems, or "bugs" as they are called, in computer programs. Suppose we had mistakenly written our program thus:

```
1  INPUT T
2  INPUT S
3  D = S * T
4  PRINT D
5  GOTO 3
```

The error is in statement 5, where we have written GOTO 3 instead of GOTO 1. Since the computer doggedly follows our program whether it makes sense or not, it goes to step 3, computes S * T, then goes to step 4 and prints the answer, and then to step 5, which tells it to return to step 3 and start over again. Since our GOTO 3 command bypasses steps 1 and 2, there is never any opportunity to enter new values for T and S. So the computer just loops around and around, printing out the same answer over and over until we shut it off or it breaks down.

In our program we have a clue that something is wrong because we see the same answer being displayed over and over on the screen. But suppose we had also made the mistake of leaving out statement 4, so that our program becomes

1   INPUT T
2   INPUT S
3   D = S * T
4   GOTO 3

Now the program circles endlessly from 3 to 4 and then back to 3 with no visible output. The computer is doing something, but what it is doing is a complete waste of time; and because there is no printed output, it may not be obvious for some time that the computer is doing useless work. Today's big, fast computers cost hundreds of dollars per hour to operate; so "bugs" like these in a program are not only annoying but can be very costly.

According to historical accounts, Lord Byron's daughter Augusta Ada was the first person to write a computer program—for a computer that was never built. In modern times the honor seems to go to Commodore Grace Murray Hopper of the United States Navy. Commodore Hopper wrote the first program for the Mark I computer, which was built, we recall, with mechanical relays. In a later version of this computer, Mark II, a moth flew into one of the relays, where it was crushed, causing the computer to stop. This, according to Commodore Hopper, was the first instance of a "bug" in program—or more correctly, in a computer.

In this case it was a simple matter to "debug" the computer with a pair of tweezers, but computer programmers agree that there is no such thing as a completely debugged program—at least not any complex program. Such a program includes so many steps, and so many different paths that the program might take, that it is impossible to check every possible computation or path. In the early days of computers, the cost of a computer usually exceeded by several times the cost of writing the program—or "software" as it is called, in contrast to the "hardware," which is the computing machine itself. Today just the opposite is true—the cost and effort to produce software is always greater, and the situation grows more serious each year. Perhaps intelligent computers will one day write their own software; in the meantime, programming remains a large and constant challenge.

7.
The Anatomy of a Computer

We know by now that all digital computers have the same basic parts. Every computer, for example, has a central processing unit (CPU) that carries out the arithmetic operations—the part Babbage called the mill. It also has a memory—Babbage's store. And it has a device for "inputting" information—perhaps a keyboard or a sensor that admits a signal from a satellite relaying information from a weather station to a weather forecast center—and a device for "outputting" information, such as a video display screen or a printer. Finally, it must have a bus to carry information from one part of the computer to another, and gates that transfer and control this flow of information.

Computers may be relatively simple or extremely complex, depending on the tasks they are designed to perform. The biggest and fastest computers cost millions of dollars and are used for complex problems like forecasting the weather or modeling world population patterns. They are located in large scientific laboratories such as the National Oceanic and Atmospheric Environmental Research Laboratories in Boulder, Colorado, and the Los Alamos National Laboratory at Los Alamos, New Mexico.

Somewhat smaller computers, called "minicomputers," are used by businesses, local government units such as cities

The technician at the terminal is operating the large Cyber 170 computer housed in cupboard-like cases in the background.

and counties, and small manufacturing plants. The smallest and least expensive computers are called "microcomputers" because the CPU—perhaps along with some other components—is contained entirely on one small chip. These computers cost from a few thousand dollars to less than one hundred dollars, and include the computers that are appearing more and more commonly in homes, offices, and schools. Since all digital computers, from the biggest to the smallest, have essentially the same parts and operate in much the same

A student operates a microcomputer system: keyboard, display screen, printer (left) and computer (right).

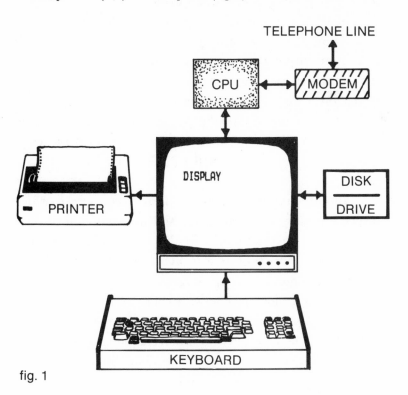

fig. 1

way, we shall concentrate on the anatomy of a microcomputer.

The picture shows a typical microcomputer. To help us understand its anatomy more clearly, we have made a diagram, Figure 1, that shows its various parts. Often most of these parts are packaged neatly in the same "box," but not always, and we have separated them here so that we can study them more easily.

First we see a *keyboard,* similar to an ordinary typewriter keyboard, for typing information or instructions into the computer. Other input devices are possible. A microcomputer installed in a car, for example, might receive information from sensors placed throughout the car to monitor oil pressure, engine temperature, automatic transmission fluid level, gasoline reserves, and so on.

In the figure we also see a device called a *disk drive,* which represents one form of memory for the computer. It is also an output device because information generated by the computer can be transferred to the disk drive and stored on a disk. These plastic disks, often called "floppy disks" because they are pliable like a piece of thin cardboard or bristol board, are normally a little less than 6 inches in diameter and resemble a small LP record for use on a turntable.

Another output device is the *video display screen,* which displays, usually in green letters and numbers, information generated by the computer. Often we want a permanent record of this information; so a *printer* is attached to our computer to provide "hard copy" as it is called.

More and more people with computers want to "talk" to other people with computers. That is, they want their computer to be connected to other computers. Quite often this is done by using the regular telephone lines. The signals generated by computers, however, cannot travel over phone lines. So another device, called a *modem,* converts signals generated by the computer into a form that can travel over phone lines.

Users with special needs may have other devices connected to their computer. They may need a device for plotting graphs, for example, or a "joystick" to move a pointer around on the display screen. Joysticks are a common feature of devices that turn television sets into video game boards.

Figure 2 is a schematic diagram of our microcomputer that gives more detailed information about its parts. Some of the parts we recognize—the CPU, bus, and keyboard. Others—the System ROM and RAM—are less familiar.

How does a computer "get going" before we have programmed it—or more likely, before we have transferred a program written earlier from a disk into the computer memory? A computer without a program is like an orchestra without music; everyone is ready to play, but no one knows what.

A computer "knows" certain things before it has been programmed, just as the orchestra musicians know, before they have seen the music, that when the conductor lowers his baton it is time to start playing. Musicians know this because

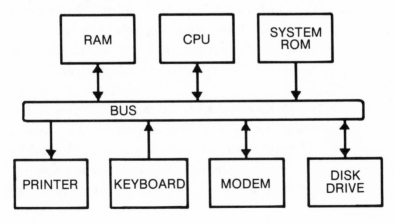

fig. 2

they carry a "permanent program" in their heads, which was "installed" when they took music lessons.

Computers also have built into them, at the factory, some permanent memory—just enough to "get things off the ground." This permanent memory is located in a device called a ROM, which stands for "read-only memory." This means that information stored in a ROM can only be "read" by the computer into its memory section, and that information generated by the computer cannot be stored in ROM. We can think of a ROM as a book from which a computer can read but in which there is no room for it to write notes in the margin and no blank pages at the back of the book for more lengthy comments.

Let's look at Figure 2 to follow what happens when we turn on the computer. First we notice that there is a box labeled System ROM, which we have just mentioned. Mainly it contains a short program which, when we turn on the computer, is sent to the CPU, telling it to look for another program called the *operating system*.

Commonly the operating system is stored on a disk; so this disk must be placed in the *disk drive* when the computer is first turned on. Usually there is room on the disk for several programs, including the operating system. The operating system is a kind of "traffic controller" that manages the devices attached to the computer, such as the disk drive and the printer. It also manages the internal operations of the computer.

Computers need operating systems because they can do only one thing at a time. A computer cannot, for example, do two arithmetic operations at the same time. Without an operating system, a computer is like a centipede whose legs all moved independently of each other—neither makes much progress.

After the operating system has been transferred to the

computer's memory, we can store other programs in the computer. These are the programs that solve the problems we are interested in—perhaps a program for computing interest on a loan, or one for editing manuscripts.

As the computer reads the operating system—or any other program—from a disk, it stores the program in its internal memory, labeled RAM in Figure 2. RAM stands for "random access memory." The main difference between RAM and ROM is that RAM is like a book with many blank pages on which we can record information and from which both we and the computer can later read this information. We can also erase the information in RAM when it is no longer needed, or when we need to make room for other information.

Another important feature of RAM is that, as its name implies, it can be accessed randomly. We can think of RAM as an array of pigeon holes, each hole having its own address. If our RAM had a hundred pigeon holes, the addresses of the holes could be the numbers 1 through 100. In each of these holes we could store a piece of information. For example, the pigeon hole at address 23 might have the letter "Q" stored in it. When the computer wants to retrieve the information from pigeon hole 23—the letter Q—it can go straight to the hole at that address without looking in holes 1 through 22 until it comes to hole 23.

This system is quite different from one in which information is stored on a magnetic tape, where we have to move the tape backward or forward until we reach the location on the tape where the piece of information we want is stored. Storage on a tape is called "serial storage." It's easy to see that it takes a computer a lot longer to find information stored serially than it does to find information stored in RAM. Unfortunately, with the present technology, information stored in RAM disappears when the computer power is interrupted or turned off; so it's important always to transfer essential information stored in RAM to a disk before turning off the computer.

Let's look more closely at how information is stored in RAM. As we have said, computers work entirely with 0's and 1's. So how can we store something like a person's name or birth date in RAM? Well, suppose we have a deck of cards, and on each card there is a letter of the alphabet—26 cards in all. If we wished our cards to be marked with both small and capital letters, we would need 52 cards; and if we wanted the numbers 0 through 9, we would need 10 more cards, or 62 cards. But then there are commas, periods, question marks, dollar signs, hyphens, quotation marks, and so on. So let's imagine that our deck contains 256 cards, which should be enough to represent almost any symbol we might wish.

Let's also imagine that the 256 cards are always in a certain order. Perhaps the order is a, b, c, d . . . A, B, C, D . . . 0, 1, 2, 3 . . . and so on, out to the last card, which might be marked with a dollar sign. How could we locate a particular card in our deck of 256 cards?

One way would be to number the cards 1 through 256, so that the letter "a" was on card 1, the letter "b" on card 2, and so on. Using our cards we could "write" the word *add* as 1, 4, 4, since these are the numbers, or *locations* in computer jargon—of the cards bearing the letters a, d, d.

But this won't work in a computer because a computer knows only two numbers—0 and 1. What can we do? Well, suppose we want to designate the card that is at location 3— the letter "c." We could ask, Is the letter "c" in the first half of the deck? If the answer is yes, we write down a number 1. If the answer is no, we write down 0. Since "c" is in the first half of the deck, we write down 1. Next we ask, Is "c" in the first half of the remaining top half of the deck? Since the answer is yes, we write down another 1.

If we continue this procedure, always asking if the letter we want to identify is in the top half of the remaining cards that contain the desired card, we will always be able to identify the position of the card after just 8 questions. That is, we will have a unique sequence of 0's and 1's that will identify each symbol in our 256-card deck. You can easily demonstrate for yourself that the letter "c" in this scheme is represented by 11111101; and the dollar sign, the last card in the deck, by 00000000.

Computer scientists call the symbols 0 and 1 "bits" of information, and a string of 8 bits is called a "byte." One byte can represent a single number or a letter of the alphabet.

RAM consists of a huge number of electronic switches located on a chip. Each switch is either *on* or *off*. If it is *on,* the normal practice is to say that the switch represents a 1; and if it is *off,* a 0. In today's computer a typical chip holds 65,536 bits of information, or 1024 bytes of information. Since it takes one byte to represent one letter of the alphabet, a single chip could store about 200 words whose average length is 5 letters. Most microcomputers have several memory chips; so they can store much more than 200 words. In the future a typical chip will hold a million or so bits of information.

Returning to Figure 2, we see that the various components of the computer—the CPU, RAM, ROM, and so on—and the input and output devices such as the keyboard and printer, are all connected to the bus, which is, as we've said, the path over which the commands and data flow. The bus is like a street along which only one vehicle can travel at a time. This is one reason computers do one thing at a time; otherwise, we would have bits colliding in the bus. These kinds of computers are called "von Neumann" computers because they are modeled along lines first suggested by John von Neumann, the previously mentioned Hungarian mathematician who developed the idea of storing a program in a computer. Future computers will be able to do several things at once; we shall discuss this "parallel processing," as it is called, in more detail later.

The heart of the computer is the CPU because this is where the information entering the computer is manipulated and transformed. We have discussed briefly how AND and OR gates can be assembled to perform various functions such as adding, subtracting, and controlling certain activities. The CPU is a maze of AND and OR gates, and one other kind of gate—the NOR gate. The NOR gate does one simple thing; it changes 1's to 0's and 0's to 1's.

One of the remarkable things that the English mathematician Alan Turing was able to do in his study of paper computers was to show that AND, OR, and NOR gates assembled in various arrays could perform any conceivable mathematical operation. His demonstration was a classic example of taking a complex machine and breaking it down into a few basic components. Of course, as we saw in our earlier analogy with the bricks, the price we have to pay for this reduction to basic building blocks is a complicated assemblage of blocks to perform the necessary functions. And it is here again that chips have come to the rescue because they allow us to pack thousands of AND, OR, and NOR gates onto a single chip. Next we shall see how chips are put to work to help us understand the world.

8.
Putting the World in a Computer

We have seen how scientists built models to help themselves understand the world. Models that predicted the movements of the sun and stars or the behavior of an airplane that had not yet been constructed we described as analog computers because they mimicked the activity of the thing the scientists wished to study.

Digital computers, too, can be used to model the world, and this is today one of the most important uses for computers. When we were discussing computer programming, we used the simple equation $D = S * T$ to determine how far a car moves at speed S when it has been traveling for T hours. Mathematical equations of this kind represent one of the most convenient and compact ways we know to model or describe our world. They allow us to calculate the path of a spaceship on its way to the moon, the strength of a television signal at different distances from the transmitter, or the chances of holding the winning number in a lottery. Any time we can model some part of our world with an equation, we can use digital computers to help us with the mathematics, whether it is simply multiplying time by speed to get distance or solving complex equations of space travel or finding the bending point of a steel beam in a skyscraper.

But we can also use digital computers to build models of things we wish to study in somewhat the same way that we used analog computers to build models. In these digital computer models, however, the parts of the model are built from numbers and data, rather than from electrical components that were wired together in just the right way in an analog computer to represent an airplane or a submarine.

As an example, let's consider a model of a library—a school library, perhaps. Such a library consists of books, magazines, and other kinds of information. One of the main activities of the library is to lend books—and to get them back. Most libraries have a card catalog that contains a file of all the books in the library. Usually there is one card for each book, and the card gives information about the book—its title, author, publisher, date of publication, and probably some indication of the book's contents. In many libraries there are two card catalogs: one lists the books alphabetically by the authors' last names and by titles; the other lists *subjects* alphabetically—Architecture, Ceramics, Education, and so on—with book titles and authors listed alphabetically under the appropriate subject or subjects.

In a way, these catalogs are a model of the library because looking through them to find out what books are in the library gives the same information as actually sorting through all of the bookshelves. And the card catalog search is a lot easier and more efficient.

The card catalog has several important characteristics of any model. First, it is a simplification of the thing it models; the cards do not contain the whole contents of the books, but just an indication of the contents. Second, the model is accurate; the card catalog should have a card for each book in the library, and should not include cards for any books the library does not have. Third, the model is easier to manipulate than the thing it models. It is much easier to go through the card catalog looking for books on dinosaurs or model airplane building than it is to look through all the books in the library—or even those in a specific section of the library.

Another characteristic of the library is that it is dynamic; people remove and return books all the time. To help keep track of the books in the system we are describing, each book has on the inside of the back cover an envelope that contains a card with the book's title and author, as well as spaces for the borrower's name or his library card number. There is also space on the card for the librarian to stamp a date when the book is to be returned. The librarian places this card in a file of books charged out to patrons. This file is a model of "who has what books checked out and when they are due." As books are returned, the cards are removed from this file and replaced in the books.

By now it should be evident that a library is a prime candidate for modeling on a computer; and today most public libraries of any size—and many smaller libraries also—do use computers in just this way. All the information in the card catalog, for example, can be put in the computer's memory; but once is enough. We don't need to enter the same information twice—once for the list of books by title, and again by author. Furthermore, we need not be concerned with the order in which we enter the books in the computer's memory. We can just enter the book titles and authors in any order that is convenient—and add new books as we acquire them. Then if we want a list of the books arranged alphabetically by title, we simply write a program that tells the computer to sort through the titles and print them alphabetically. Or we could write a program that lists alphabetically all books by a certain author.

Or if for some reason we wished to do such a thing, we

could write a program to list only those books that had titles
with the words "black cats" or "brown beans" in the title—
or even only those books with the words "black, cats, brown,
beans" (in any order) in their titles. The list would doubtless be very short.

The ability to "slice through" the computer's memory
in almost any way we please to assemble information is one
of the most powerful advantages of computer-stored information. Let's consider the possibilities further, and go beyond
storing just authors and titles in computer memory. We can
imagine the advantages of having an entire encyclopedia
stored in a computer; this would let us quickly pull together
bits of information from throughout the whole encyclopedia.
The way we work with an encyclopedia now, we may have
to look through many unwieldy volumes to assemble the information we want—and we may still not succeed because the
index to the encyclopedia may not be "fine" enough in detail
to reveal some obscure point we are trying to search out.

You may recall quite vividly, for example, that somewhere, sometime, you saw a list of the chemicals that make
up the human body, and their value in dollars. You wish to
use this information in a paper for your science class, but
where can you find it now?

When a computer searches through its memory, every
word in the encyclopedia is in the "index." So you might enter such key words as "chemistry," "chemicals," and "human
body." You remember that calcium, phosphorus, and iron,
and perhaps one or two other specific chemicals are in the
body; so you enter these, too. Then you send the computer
searching through the encyclopedia in its memory to assemble the needed information.

Of course, the encyclopedia may not contain the specific
information you are looking for, but the computer will
quickly tell you this, and you can stop wasting time looking

in that source and look elsewhere. We can imagine that not just the encyclopedia, but the entire contents of the library are stored in computer memory. In a way we are now at a point where the information in the computer is no longer a model of the library—it *is* the library.

Now we can assemble information on any subject from all the books in the library, and we can display it on video screens or print it out on high-speed printers or send it over telephone lines to other libraries that need the information because it is not in their store of information—all without moving from our chair in front of the computer. We haven't quite reached this point yet, but disks similar to LP records are already available in the experimental stage that can store small libraries on a single disk, and the entire Library of Congress on a few dozen disks.

But let's return to a somewhat less elegant version of a library to see some of the other characteristics of model building with computers. We have said that a library is dynamic; books are taken out and returned; new books are ordered; some books are lost, and some destroyed or stolen; others need to be replaced or repaired. But a library is more than books. There are the people who use the library and the people who work there. A city library may be busier in the summer than in winter, whereas a college library may be little used in the summer because of smaller summertime enrollment.

If a computer were keeping track of the number of persons using the library each month during the year, the information could be used to help decide when temporary help was needed to cope with heavy library use; or use trends over the years could help predict when the library needed to be expanded or when perhaps it would be advisable to build a branch library.

But then the city may not have unlimited resources to

build or expand the library, and it may be desirable to model *all* of the city's important activities on a computer—everything from street construction and repair to running the water system and the police and fire departments. If we consider all the activities and parts that go to make up a community, and all the interactions that may take place among the various parts, we soon reach the point where no single human mind— or collection of minds—could juggle enough facts about changing and interacting components at one time to comprehend what was going on.

If we build a new community art and concert center, what will be the impact on the library expansion? Offhand it would seem that there is only so much money to do only so many things; so if funds are limited, expanding the library may have to be done at the expense of starting an art and concert center. But then a realistic model of a city that includes tax collection, tourist attractions, highway expenditures, and so on might predict, when studied on a computer, that a new art and concert center would attract enough new tourists—who pay city sales tax along with everybody else— to pay for the library expansion and make a good start on the art and concert center.

Computers are very good at keeping a multitude of facts "in mind" at once, and following in infinite detail what happens "here" if you do such-and-such "there." But there is one big catch—and it is a very big catch indeed: if the model is bad and the information that goes into the computer is bad, then the predictions will be bad. "Garbage in—garbage out," as computer users say.

Today computers are used to model everything from the weather to global warfare. But the usefulness of such endeavors will never be any better than the fidelity of the models and the information that goes into them. We may have a very good model for world-wide weather patterns. But if we put the wrong data—wrong temperatures, atmospheric pressures, and other weather facts—into the computer, then the weather forecasts may be worse than useless. Or even if the weather data are accurate, the wrong model will never provide useful information.

We have observed, however, that computers are versatile, and poor models can be corrected. If we believe that the data our model depends on are accurate, and if we find that the forecasts the model makes are wrong, then we can change the model, and keep on changing it, until finally it does "work." Model building on computers helps us test our ideas about how the world works. We can literally put the world in a computer. And with the computer we can speed up the march of time a thousand and even a million fold, to see what is around the corner—even before we know there is a corner. Model building is so important that we shall continue our investigation of its advantages and limitations in the next chapter.

9.
White Boxes, Black Boxes, and Gray Boxes

Perhaps you've had the experience of watching a salesperson demonstrating some gadget like a "new" kitchen knife that does everything from slicing pickles to producing intricate garnishes from carrots, celery, and other vegetables. It seems very easy as the demonstrator explains how "you too" can get the same wonderful results with his new $5.95 knife. But when you buy the knife you realize that it is practically like every other knife in your kitchen, and that what the salesperson had was not an exceptional knife but exceptional skill in using a knife.

It is not always easy to know what is skill and what is machine. When we hear that computers guide space vehicles to the moon or control operations in an automobile assembly plant, we have the "knife-skill" problem: what part is due to the inherent power of the computer, and what was due to the skill of the persons who programmed the computer? Let's explore the distinction between machine and program, with emphasis in this chapter on the limitations of programming; later we'll look at the ways in which computers are limited.

Why is it important to gain a good understanding of programming, the skill side of the knife-skill problem? First, because some of our fear and mistrust of computers come from the fact that we imagine that a sufficiently powerful computer, coupled with the right program and given enough time, could do almost anything—a very disturbing thought. And second, because when we develop some feeling for what programs can and cannot do, we will not waste our time and effort working on projects that will never yield a useful answer.

There are many different kinds of programs that we might study to gain insight into the relationship between machines and programs. Since we've already learned a little bit about the idea of model building on computers, let's use model building as a way to investigate the machine-skill problem. The spectrum of different kinds of models exposes clearly the many problems a programmer meets when he starts to build a model.

We have considered basically two kinds of models. One was a simple equation for determining distances, and the other was a model of a library, expanded, finally, to include the whole city. Model building is certainly on the skill side of the machine-skill coin. The model, however, may be so intricate that the computer at hand doesn't have enough memory to contain the entire model; or the computer may be too slow to produce an answer in a reasonable length of time. But these are different problems, related to the machine side of the coin. What we're interested in now is the skill side.

When we look at model building, the equation for distance traveled by a vehicle moving at a certain speed ($D = S * T$) seems simple enough. There's not much room for argument here. A model of a city, on the other hand, provides room for endless controversy. What should be included in the model, and what should be left out? Is it enough to consider just the main streets, or should every side street and alley be included? If we include every detail, the computer may have to run for days before it "comes to any conclusion."

Aside from concerns of this kind, there are concerns having to do with value judgments: should money be provided to buy pieces of art for the new city hall? Should the schools allocate more money for counseling students at the expense of buying more computers for those taking business and math courses? We can see that decisions having to do with value judgments should not be left to machines. Computers may provide us with information to help make these decisions, but *computers have only the values we build into them.*

Returning to $D = S * T$, is there more that we can say about this simple equation? Yes, quite a bit more. First, we can look at it from different points of view. In our first encounter with the equation, we asked what distance a vehicle travels if we know its speed and time of travel. But the equation can also be rewritten to tell us how long a vehicle has been on the road if we know its speed and the distance it has come. If we know, for example, someone has traveled 150 miles at a constant speed of 50 miles per hour, we know he has been on the road for 3 hours. In this case, to find the travel time we rewrite our equation as $T = D$ divided by S. Or using the symbol for "divide" used on most computer keyboards, we would write $T = D/S$.

Similarly, if we know that someone has been on the road for 3 hours and has traveled 150 miles, we know that his average speed is 50 miles per hour, or in terms of our equation, $S = D/T$.

We notice that if we know any two of the quantities involved in our equation, we can always figure out the third. Figure 1 demonstrates this fact. At the top of the diagram we see a box into which the values for speed, S, and time, T, are entered; and exiting from the box is the distance, D. In the

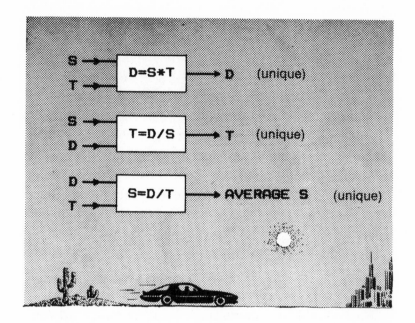

fig. 1

middle box, S and D are entered, and T emerges. And in the bottom box, S emerges when D and T are entered.

We could think of the boxes as simple computers that perform the operation S * T in the first box, D/S in the second, and D/T in the third. So what we can say about this particular problem is that given any two of the three quantities, we can always figure out the third, and that the quantity figured out is "unique." That is, if we know that S is 10 miles per hour and that T is one hour, then D will always be 10 miles—not 11 miles one time and 14 some other time.

Another thing we can say is that we know exactly what goes on in the boxes. Looking at the top box, for example, we know that it multiplies S by T. These are not "black boxes," where something mysterious goes on, but "white boxes," whose internal workings are completely known to us.

White boxes represent one end of the spectrum of model building because we can model what goes on inside them exactly, with no uncertainties. At the other end of the spectrum are black boxes because we can only guess what goes on inside. The human brain is nearly a black box because we know little of what goes on inside.

Somewhere in the middle are "gray boxes." In gray boxes we have some knowledge of what goes on, but our knowledge is not complete. A model of the earth's weather "machine" is a gray box because we are fairly certain about some features—most of the equations governing atmospheric motions, for example—but the role played by the interaction between the oceans and the atmosphere is less well understood.

Figure 2 represents a kind of "idealized box" that may be black or white or some shade of gray between black and white. There may be several inputs to the box and several outputs. The box itself we have labeled "B," which means simply that whatever goes on in the box is carried out here.

In most "box" problems, as in the equations involving D, S, and T, we know two things, such as the inputs and B; and we want to determine a third—in this case, the outputs. For example, if the inputs are S and T and we know that the box performs the operation S * T, then we know that the output is D.

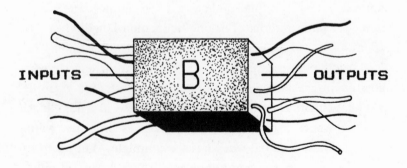

INPUTS   B   OUTPUTS

fig. 2

Systems like this, in which we know the inputs and what the box does—that is, we know B—almost always yield a definite result. Most electronic devices are of this nature—a TV set, for example. If we know what signal goes into the TV set from the antenna, then we know exactly what the output—the picture on the screen—will be because we know what the System B is. That is, we know what goes on inside the TV set because we designed it.

The inverse of this situation is not necessarily true, however. To go back to Figure 1, if we know that the output of the box is D and that the box performs the operation $S * T$, we don't have unique values for S and T. If D is 100 miles, then any combination of S and T that when multiplied together gives 100 miles is acceptable: 20 miles per hour times 5 hours, or 100 miles per hour times 1 hour, and so on.

Most devices having to do with control are of this type in which we know B and the outputs, and we want to determine some combination of the inputs that will yield the correct result. For example, a pilot guiding an airplane through a storm has to do a good deal of maneuvering of the controls in the cockpit to keep the plane on a steady path. Here we know B, how the plane reacts to various changes of the controls in the cockpit; and we know the outputs because we know the corrective actions taken by the pilot. The question is what gusts of wind and other factors—the inputs—required the pilot to take precisely the corrective actions that he took.

The third and last possibility is that we know the inputs and outputs, and we want to know B. Studying the human brain is a good example. If you smile at somebody, he or she will probably smile back. What went on in the brain to bring about this result? There are probably about as many answers to the question as there are persons who think about it—and many of them may be correct because different people often do the same thing for different reasons.

These kinds of problems are usually referred to as "black box problems" because the problem is to figure out what is in the box—or more correctly, Can we think of some mechanism—any mechanism—in the box that will produce the correct output for the known input? At some future time it may be impossible to tell, over a phone line, whether you are speaking to a computer or to another person. But this does not mean that the way the computer works is identical to the working of the human brain.

We are beginning to see that modeling has a lot of different dimensions. The box may range from white to black, and we may know inputs and not outputs, or vice versa; or we may know only inputs and outputs, and know from everything to next to nothing about the box. As we said, electronic devices—and many other devices that we design and manufacture—tend to be white boxes. Then as we move into the gray area, we have things like experimental aircraft that we may know something about, because we design them, but that may have some uncertainties because we don't know, for example, just how certain wing structures interact with the air at high speeds. Generally in these kinds of problems the box is not so gray that we give up the notion of obtaining reliable technical results.

On the other hand, models of genetic engineering or air pollution are moving into a much grayer area. In studying air pollution, for example, we are uncertain as to what processes are important in the atmosphere, and we may not even have instruments capable of gathering the right kind of data. But still the problem is well enough understood that we expect to get at least some specific results.

It's when we get into areas of economics and politics that the box really begins to turn black. Here the laws are barely understood, if at all; and equally disconcerting, no one is even certain as to which elements are important and which are not. But this does not mean that computer models are of no help in these areas because, as we have seen, computers can deal with many interacting components at once; so models can on many occasions provide us with trends or "rules of thumb," if not complete answers.

As we have said, building models on computers is just one kind of computer activity. But in any of these activities, as in model building, the computer cannot make up for deep inadequacies or uncertainties. And once more it's a situation of garbage in, garbage out. Now that we understand something about computer limitations from the programming point of view, we have a clearer idea of some of the difficulties programmers must cope with, and we can see that even the best programs can't make computers omniscient or omnipotent.

10.
Hidden Computers That Talk Out Loud

Children are often more eager to try new inventions and embrace new technologies than adults are. In archeological digs, toys with wheels have been found that predate by hundreds of years man's first serious attempts to use wheels for transportation. Older generations, perhaps because they feel comfortable with the "old ways," or perhaps because they mistrust and are a little frightened by the new ways, tend to cling to what is familiar to them. This same situation has occurred with computers. Small children bang away at a computer keyboard that intimidates their parents or teachers, seemingly knowing what to do with little or no outside help. To them the computer is just another toy to explore and enjoy.

Toys are a nonthreatening way to introduce new technologies because people feel no need to take a toy seriously. The whole business of invention and technological innovation is, in fact, as much game playing as anything else. And those inventors who play the game best seem never to lose their child-like sense of wonder and joy at discovering something just for the fun of it.

Computers rapidly invaded the world of children and

teenagers—and finally adults, too—in the form of video games. The first video games used expensive computers, and appeared only in waiting areas of places like restaurants and airports or in amusement arcades. But the relentless pace in the advancement of electronics soon spawned the development of devices that could turn ordinary television sets into home video games.

At first these were electronic versions of familiar competitions like baseball and auto racing; many children had owned electric football and basketball games powered by ordinary flashlight batteries, and they welcomed the more exciting electronic versions. But soon these were pushed aside by new games created entirely for the new medium of computer-controlled game playing. Pac-Man is a good example.

Inexpensive computers on a chip have also found places in other kinds of toys, from toy robots that can make their way through obstacle courses to toys that teach children how to spell. These computerized spelling teachers have endless patience. They not only pronounce the words the child is to spell, but tell him or her politely—in a voice that seems to come from a hollow pipe—when the pupil has made a mistake. The more advanced spelling teachers even keep track of the words the pupil most often misspells, and then keep sneaking these back into the pupil's work until he or she knows them "letter perfect."

The same sequence of events that marked the growing use of computers in toys has characterized their more serious uses. Business people first used computers to do what they had formerly done by hand, or with mechanical and later electric machines—accounting, inventory control, solving equations. But as people began to realize more fully the potential capabilities of computers, they started to use them for things man had never done and could not have done before. Things like guiding men to land on the moon and solving equations that a million mathematicians working for a million years could not have solved.

The computerized voices that first spoke in children's games later appeared in the adult world. We have computerized voices in our cars that tell us to fasten our seat belts or that we have left our lights on, or that the fuel supply is dangerously low. Computerized voices at automatic bank teller windows greet us with a cheerful "Good morning" and then tell us that we have inserted our teller card incorrectly or that we have used an unacceptable identification number. And when we dial a telephone number that has been changed to a new number, we are told that the "old number 559-7743 has been changed to 645-8923." Anyone who has heard one of these telephone messages knows that the voice sounds much like a human voice, but the speech has a halting quality—a clue that a computer is doing the talking.

Computers "dedicated" to a special function like providing a computerized voice or monitoring and outputting information about oil pressure and brake fluid condition in our cars are, of course, much less visible than all-purpose computers that "stand alone" like a typewriter or telephone. Sometimes we may not even know that our new camera is computer controlled or that a computer in a microwave oven computes cooking times for various kinds of food and tells us when the corn is cooked "just right."

In contrast to the all-purpose computer that is a complete machine, the special-purpose "hidden" computer is only one small piece of the system in which it's used. A computerized camera, for example, has all the parts of a regular camera—lens, shutter, film advance, and so on—plus a microcomputer that adjusts the focus, shutter speed, et cetera after "reading" light conditions, distance to the main object in the picture, and other inputs.

The tiny computer that imitates human speech is also a

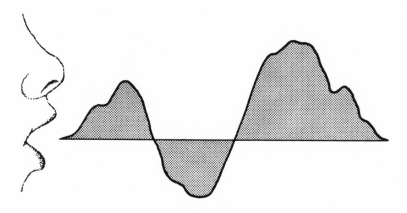

fig. 1   Continuous sound wave

hidden part of a larger system. Research into computerized speech is one of the fastest-growing areas of interest in the computer industry, and no single approach has won out. Two forms of speech synthesis, however, have received the most attention—modeled and unmodeled. The unmodeled form is the easier to understand, so we'll discuss it first.

Let's imagine reading into a tape recorder all the words in an ordinary English dictionary—one containing 100,000 words, let's say. This would take one person about 100 working days, since most people speak at the rate of about 200 words per minute. Then suppose we cut the tape into 100,000 pieces, with each piece containing the voice pattern of one word. We could then create speech by assembling the pieces in an order that corresponds to the sentence we wish to make, glue the pieces together, and play the tape back. In actual practice, the sounds of the 100,000 words could be stored in ROM, using a process called "analog to digital conversion." How does the process work?

Well, if we could see a sound wave, it would look something like the pattern shown in Figure 1. Different words, of course, would have different patterns. As we know, digital computers can store information only in strings of 0's and

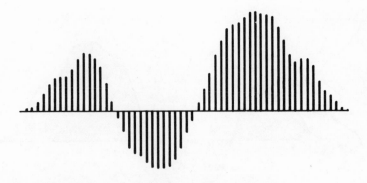

fig. 2   Sound wave converted to discreet spikes

1's. To translate our words into strings of 0's and 1's, we first break up the continuous sound wave into a series of discrete signals, as shown in Figure 2. We can see by comparing the two figures that the discrete version of the sound wave preserves the pattern of the continuous wave.

Next we convert the height of each of the discrete components of the sound wave into a number; the taller the "spike," the bigger the number we assign to it. We now have a long string of numbers whose values increase or decrease according to the pattern of the original sound wave.

The next step is to convert the string of numbers into an even longer string of binary digits by following the same process described in Chapter 7. That is, we use a discrete string of 0's and 1's to represent each digit, and then store them in ROM. We now have our 100,000-word dictionary in ROM, where it can be accessed by a computer.

Next we need a computer program to assemble words stored in ROM to build sentences. There are several ways to do this, but one simple way is to have a program that searches out from ROM whatever word we type on the computer keyboard. If we type the word *clock,* for example, the program retrieves from ROM the string of bits that represents the word *clock.*

Next the bits are sent to an electronic device that converts the bits back to the numbers representing the spikes as shown in Figure 2, and finally another circuit converts the spikes back to a continuous wave form that looks like the original wave shown in Figure 1. This process is, of course, just the reverse of the process we used to transform the continuous wave form into bits.

Now that we have the original wave form—usually as an electrical signal—back for the word *clock,* we can send the signal to a speaker that will reproduce the sound as originally recorded on tape.

All of this happens so fast that it seems to the human mind and ear to be instantaneous. But there are two problems with this approach. First, speech as we know it is more than just a string of words assembled in an intelligible order. The same word is voiced differently, depending on its position in a sentence and the meaning of the sentence. Consider the two sentences, "This is my homework." and "This is my homework?" These sentences, when spoken, have entirely different meaning, easily discernible to the listener by the way the words sound. We show this difference in writing by using a period to end the statement and a question mark to end the question. This problem of the same words sounding different depending on how they're used has not yet been solved in computer speech. It partially accounts for the halting quality of the computerized telephone announcements.

The second problem is that the amount of memory required to store our dictionary in ROM is costly; something like ten trillion bits would have to be stored. By today's standards, even a million bits stored in ROM is a lot. This problem has been overcome to some extent by using various mathematical tricks to simplify the patterns of sounds, but much more work still needs to be done.

The other approach—the model approach—is to build a

computer model of the human voice. Let's consider first, not a computer model, but a mechanical model for speech. Our model might consist of a bellows to produce puffs of air, a vibrating reed to produce sounds as the puffs of air strike it, and a chamber whose shape could be changed to resemble the changes in the lips, tongue, and mouth cavity as we speak. This mechanical "speaking machine" could be operated somewhat like a player piano. A series of holes in the "piano roll," laid out in a pattern, would operate the machine, causing it to huff and puff and move its "mouth" to produce words. Such machines have in fact been built to produce recognizable words. It's not too hard to imagine that we could build an electronic version of this machine, since electronic organs that simulate the sound of pipe organs have been on the market for several decades. In our electronic speaking machine, however, the "piano roll" is replaced by a computer program. The big advantage to this scheme is that we can create almost any sound we wish with the appropriate program; we are not stuck with a restricted set of sounds or words as we were in the "dictionary approach."

How much information does it take to operate such a machine? Well, it turns out that if the program feeds the machine information at the rate of 5000 bits per second, then intelligible but peculiar-sounding speech is produced. Using this approach, a ROM programmed to "speak out" the entire contents of our 100,000-word dictionary would need about one one-hundredth as much storage capacity as the ROM needed in our dictionary approach.

Although computerized speech does not approximate the quality of human speech, the models are becoming better and better. Perhaps model building is the most important benefit of today's attempts to produce computerized speech. By studying the defects in the speech produced by models, we learn how to improve these models and thus may come closer to understanding how human speech "really works."

In addition to the many makes of home computers advertised widely in newspapers and magazines and on TV and begging us to buy one and take it home, hundreds of unadvertised special-use computers are sneaking in our back doors in cameras, micro-wave ovens, and other devices without our even recognizing them. Daily we are all becoming more and more "computerized," whether we know it or not and whether we like it or not. As we continue our investigation of computers used for specialized purposes, we shall see how they can be teamed with arms and legs to make robots.

11.
Robots with
Computer Brains

The museums of Europe display elaborate "toys" of eighteenth century aristocrats. Intricate clocks announce the hour with heads and figures that pop out of windows and doors, and Lilliputian orchestras sway in unison to some classic melody. The king of the model makers, Johann Nepumuk Maelzel, even commissioned Beethoven to write the *Wellington's Victory* for his mechanical orchestra, the Panharmonium.

These imitations of ourselves fascinate, amuse, and sometimes terrify us. They act, seemingly on their own; yet their unchanging facial expressions give no clue to what they may be "thinking." Dolls that cry and talk are cute, but more serious imitations, such as Dr. Frankenstein's creation, may cause uncertainty and fear. And closer to home, workers today feel threatened by robots that weld cars and assemble electronic instruments.

The word *robot* comes from a Czech word that means "forced labor." It is this potential of robots, the possibility of using them for tedious and boring—and sometimes dangerous—tasks that makes them attractive and at the same time threatening. For decades we have had automatic machines that follow a predetermined set of operations; the automatic washing machine, for example, washes, rinses, and spin-dries our clothes. The mechanical toys of the past were the ancestors of our automatic machines, for they too went through a sequence of actions totally determined in advance by the inner arrangement of their cogs, wheels, and levers.

But robots controlled by computers are as different from automatic machines as computers are from simple calculators. Such robots do far more than merely repeat the same activity over and over. Computer-controlled robots respond to changes in their environment, and advanced robots even remember a little of their past to help them cope with the future.

The ability of machines to respond to changes in their environment has developed largely around a concept called *feedback control.* This means that a machine can "decide" what to do in the future based on the consequences of its past actions. That is, information is "fed back" to the machine so that it can determine whether it is reaching its goal, and what to do if it is not.

A thermostat to regulate the heat in a house or building is an often cited example of feedback at work. The thermostat has an external dial that we can set to the desired room temperature—say 68 degrees Fahrenheit. The thermostat also measures the actual room temperature, which might be 59 degrees. Since there is a 9-degree difference between the actual temperature and the desired temperature, the thermostat generates an electrical signal that travels along a wire to the furnace to turn it on.

As the room warms, its temperature approaches the desired temperature, 68 degrees. When this temperature is reached, the thermostat instructs the furnace to turn off. Later, as the room cools below 68 degrees, the thermostat signal turns the furnace on again, until the desired temperature is reached once more. In most thermostats the "turn on" signal is sent when the room temperature drops a degree or two below the desired temperature, so that the furnace isn't continually turning on and off.

The difference between the desired temperature and the actual room temperature is monitored continuously by the thermostat because the thermostat has the actual room temperature "fed back" to it. We could think of the difference between the actual temperature and the desired temperature as a measure of the error between the desired and the actual situation. This error, in our example, starts at 9 degrees and approaches o degrees as the room reaches the desired temperature.

In a sense, the goal of the feedback system is to reduce the error from 9 degrees to 0 degrees. That is, we can describe in exact numerical terms what the system is to do—keep the error at 0 degrees at all times. Feedback control systems have this "numerical" quality about them. It is not a question of maybe this sometimes, and something else another time—a quality more characteristic of human beings.

Robots depend heavily on feedback control because it allows them to adjust to changes in their environment. Let's consider a robot designed to shape logs into railroad ties. Logs come in different sizes, and the robot has to adjust to this fact; it can't simply shave the same amount of wood from the sides of logs, but must adjust its shaving according to the diameter of each individual log. So one of the first steps the tie-making robot must take is to measure the diameter of each log as it comes along. This information is then fed back to the robot's sawing apparatus to assure that each log is shaved by the desired amount.

It is this uncertainty about "what is coming up next" that feedback control helps to solve, and it is this ability to cope with the unexpected that gives robots with feedback control a certain "humanness."

Feedback control is not without problems, however. One of the biggest problems has to do with the stability of the system—which in turn depends on whether the feedback is negative or positive. Our thermostat is an example of negative feedback; it turns the furnace on when the room is too cold, and off when the desired room temperature is reached. Negative feedback does not allow the system to get out of control, but keeps it at some desired level.

But suppose the thermostat had been installed incorrectly, so that it turned the furnace on when the temperature was at or above the desired level and never turned the furnace on when the temperature was below the desired level. This would be an example of positive feedback because the room keeps getting hotter and hotter or colder and colder, depending on what the room temperature happened to be when the furnace was first turned on at the beginning of the winter season.

We sometimes experience the results of positive feedback in an auditorium when someone turns up the volume on the sound system and the loudspeakers suddenly start shrieking. What has happened is that as a person talks or sings into the microphone, the loudspeakers reproduce the amplified sound. Then part of this sound is fed back to the microphone and the system amplifies not only the voice at the microphone but also the sound from its own loudspeakers—which again increases the sound level at the microphone. As the system becomes overloaded, it breaks into a piercing screech. In some positive feedback systems, things don't actually "blow up" like this, but they swing wildly between two extremes. Systems with negative feedback tend to be stable, whereas those with positive feedback can become unstable.

Another problem with feedback systems has to do with "timeliness." Again turning to our thermostat, let's suppose

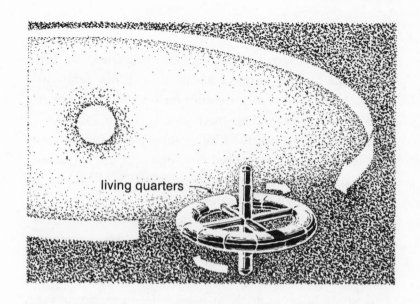

living quarters

fig. 1

it is installed in the living quarters of a doughnut-shaped space platform that revolves about its axis once per hour as it circles the sun. (See Figure 1.) The living quarters are in one small section of the doughnut, so that the windows providing light for the living quarters face the sun for a short time each hour. When the windows face the sun, intense radiation floods the living quarters, rapidly heating the rooms. But when the windows do not face the sun, the rooms cool rapidly in the darkness of outer space.

In our space ship, the thermostat turns on the electric heaters when the rooms are in darkness, and air conditioners when the rooms face the sun. But suppose the temperature control system fails, so that as the living quarters turn away from the sun, the signal to turn on the heaters reaches the heaters only after a long delay—say a delay equal to the amount of time the living quarters are out of the sun—perhaps 50 minutes each hour.

Now as the windows move out of the sun, the air conditioners stay on, accelerating the cooling of an already cooling room. Finally, as the windows revolve into the sun again, the thermostat sends out a signal to turn on the air conditioners, which are already on. The situation goes from bad to worse because the right information is received too late—another unstable situation.

People who design robots incorporating feedback have to worry about these kinds of problems. A robot making the right move at the wrong time is probably worse than no robot at all. It may try to fill paint cans on a production line after the cans have gone by, or trim logs into railroad ties according to the dimensions of the previous log.

The trouble with robots and with automation in general is that a lot of damage can be done in a short time. There are numerous tales of such machines going berserk. One involved an addressing system that automatically sorted out magazine subscribers who were due for renewal notices, printed necessary information on the notice slips, folded them, inserted them in envelopes, addressed the envelopes, and dumped them into mail sacks—all with no human help. But it was only after a human being noticed a strangely rhythmic sound coming from the machine that it was discovered that the machine had sent several hundred identical notices to the same subscriber.

Machines and robots are sometimes very strong, and if one is out of control it may endanger both itself and its human "fellow employees." One such robot with a defective component sheared off its own arm.

It is in situations like these that computers make a real contribution. They can digest a large amount of information from a number of sources and shut down the addressing system before it wastes the company's stationery and postage, or stop the paint-can-filling robot when there are no more cans on the line.

Figure 2 shows how a computer-controlled feedback system for a robot filling paint cans might work. The input to the system is the location of the paint can, and the output of the system directs the location of the paint-filling "hand" of the robot. The location of the robot's hand is fed back to a device, the *comparator,* which compares the robot's actual hand position with the location of the can. If they are different, an error signal is sent to a device—a computer—that tells the arm-hand controlling device that the hand should move to approach the paint can. The computer signal may be quite complicated if, for example, the hand has both wrist action and fingers to control.

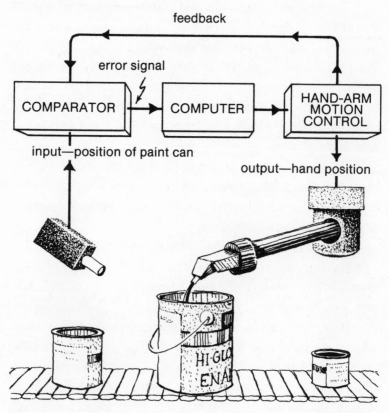

fig. 2

Feedback control has greatly extended the usefulness and reliability of machines, but still it is not enough to let robots do what human beings do. What else would be required of a more "human" robot? Well, first it should be capable of learning. If a robot is filling paint cans, it should be able to learn to put different amounts of paint into different size cans. It might learn this the hard way by putting too much paint in a new size can; it's electronic eyes would notice spilled paint. Then the next time it had to deal with this size can, it would "remember" its mistake and not make it again.

Even more subtle, the robot would learn how to learn. By this we mean that its first crude attempts at learning would be replaced later by more sophisticated ways. If it first learned to judge different size paint cans according to whether paint spilled or not, it might later incorporate information gained from its electronic eyes about the properties and volumes of shapes in space. That is, it would be able to integrate information to come up with an answer that was more accurate and obtained with less difficulty. In learning how to learn, it could also make judgments about what is worth learning and what is not.

Super-smart robots would also develop models of what they were doing, and then continually test them to improve them. Such a robot might notice that it filled cans with red barn paint more than any other kind, and that after a "siege" of filling cans with barn paint, the production line usually shut down. It would anticipate this shut-down and decide that these periods of inactivity were a good time for it to test its own internal circuitry for possible malfunctions and defects.

It might even develop a theory as to why the shut-downs occurred: during the day, when human beings like to work, they fill orders for small runs of nonstandard colors; at night the large production runs of barn paint take place, and the man in charge thinks the whole thing is very boring. So he starts the production run and soon falls asleep, awaking sometime after the run has been completed. Of course, the robot's theory may be wrong, but at least it makes his own life a little less monotonous.

At present we are a long way from the bored robot. Most robots are in the feedback stage. But as computers—the brains of the robot—and the programs that run on them become more sophisticated, we may well have to deal with bored robots—or even robots that demand better working conditions and higher wages. It may be that if we give the robot "enough brains" to build models of its work environment, this very ability will allow it to speculate about other things as well—maybe even building other robots.

In some ways it seems impossible that a robot could build a duplicate of itself. We are used to machines that turn out parts considerably less complicated than the machines that produced them. A machine to stamp out coins, for example, is considerably more complicated than a coin. It seems that there is always a loss in complexity as we go from machine to product.

John von Neumann, whom we met earlier as the inventor of the stored program, was intrigued by this problem. He was inclined to believe that robots could reproduce themselves, and perhaps even build more complicated versions of themselves. One thing that made him feel this way was his observation of nature. Obviously, nature's creatures reproduce themselves all the time. After some analysis, von Neumann was able to show, mathematically, that machines below a certain level of complexity could only produce items with reduced complexity; but machines whose complexity was above this level could produce machines of equal or greater complexity.

The explanation seems to be that it is possible, given enough rules, to generate almost unlimited complexity. Language is a good example. Languages consist of words and rules for manipulating these words. This process is sufficient to generate phrases and sentences, every day, that no one has ever heard before, and there is no end in sight. It is not as if we somehow select from a fixed storehouse of phrases and sentences those we need to express our thoughts. And besides, the brain probably does not have enough memory to hold every phrase and sentence it might ever need. Rather, we "invent" what we need as the occasion arises.

Von Neumann's analysis predated by a number of years the discovery that every creature in nature carries in its genes enough information for reproduction. So, as it turned out, his scheme for machine reproduction was probably closer to nature's scheme than even he had imagined.

But as matters stand now, robot reproduction clearly requires man in the "loop." And furthermore, a robot's "brains" are no better than the man-made program that directs the computer that directs the robot.

In the early days of programming, many persons realized that programming languages like BASIC were not very well suited for instructing robots or for simulating intelligence on computers. The problem with languages like BASIC is that every single step must be spelled out. Let's consider the problem of programming a robot to pick up a single part from a bin full of similar parts and insert the part in a hole, for example. The parts in the bin will have random positions, of course, and some of them may even be the wrong part. It would be a tremendous job to write a program in BASIC that allows for all the possible positions of the parts in the bin and to discover when the robot was dealing with a wrong part. It would be nice to have a more flexible programming language so as not to have to foresee every single possibility.

This RM III robot is demonstrating how it can be of use in an office.

Another difficulty is that programs like those written in BASIC tend to "see" everything very precisely; and when we attempt to turn concepts into precise statements, we quite often lose information. A programming language called LISP, developed in 1958, is much better suited for programming robots because it is more flexible than languages like BASIC. LISP can manipulate symbols more nearly the way human beings do; and it can also manipulate other programs to build up complex new programs. LISP is also closer to human thinking than other programming languages, in the sense that its program steps can be organized around symbols that are related. For example, if a human being had the job of picking parts from a bin and inserting them into holes, he would be thinking of the bin and the parts and the action associated with inserting the parts in the holes. This kind of association of "what needs to be done with what articles" is possible with LISP.

But still LISP can't really be the answer for causing robots to behave like human beings because it, like BASIC, is a language for computers that carry out one step at a time; and this process is not at all like the "programs" in the brain that direct the brain's many simultaneous activities. It's the speed with which computers manipulate information that sometimes makes them *seem* to operate like human beings.

Some two-hundred years ago a Hungarian inventor named Wolfgang von Kempelen astounded the world with his chess-playing robot. The robot took on all comers, and beat most of them—even master chess players. Later it was discovered that inside the "robot" was a former Polish soldier who had lost his legs in battle, and who also happened to be a champion chess player.

Had von Kempelen been alive today, he would not have needed a human chess player in his robot because any one of a number of book-size electronic chess players on the market can play at advanced levels, and large computers programmed to play chess can even beat world champions about half the time. Many computer scientists believe that we are not far from the day when the computer will always win. How do computers play the game?

In the average chess game there are about 30 legal moves that can be made each time it is a player's turn to move. For each of these 30 moves, there are about 30 responses that the player's opponent might make. So there are on the average about 30 times 30, or 900 possible moves to consider. If a player is looking one move ahead, there are 30 times 30 possible combinations of moves to consider, along with their 30 times 30 responses, or a total of about 800,000 positions to consider. We can see that if a player is looking 4 or 5 moves ahead, the number of possible moves is astronomical.

In the average chess game there are about 40 moves; so the number of possible positions a computer must consider, for just the first move, would take it about 10^{98}—that is 1 followed by 98 zeroes—years, if we had a computer that could evaluate moves at the rate of 1000 billion per second.

One of the most successful chess-playing programs, Belle, was developed at the Bell Laboratories. Belle can evaluate moves at the rate of 160,000 per second, or about 29 million positions in 3 minutes, which is the typical evaluation time between moves. Belle looks ahead 3 moves, which turns out to be about 50 times more possible moves to examine than Belle has time for in 3 minutes. She overcomes this deficiency by pruning out moves that are not worth pursuing. For example, the opponent's response to a particular move at the first level of play may be so superior that it would be a waste of time to pursue that line of attack any further. In this way, the computer does not waste time tracking down weak moves.

But is this intelligence? We certainly associate chess playing with intelligence. But then, what is intelligence? Most would argue that there is a lot more to intelligence than being able to play chess. The chess-playing program seems to win more by applying "brute force" computation than by innovative, "elegant" play. But then, maybe intelligence is nothing more than brute force computation; it's just that our conscious mind does not know what is going on "behind the scenes." And given the incredible brute-force computation power of computers, can we always expect to find an answer? Let's look at that subject next.

12.
Even Computers Can't Do Everything

An old adage says, "What one man can do, another can undo." But that may not be true—if the "doing" is making secret codes and the "undoing" is breaking them. With the use of computers, schemes have been devised that make it practically impossible to break a code—even by using another computer. "Practically impossible" doesn't mean never; it means that by the time the code is broken, no one would care. Our sun would long ago have become a cold cinder.

Simple substitution codes are easy to break; it takes only seconds with a computer. These are the kinds of codes in which one symbol is replaced by another: "a" might be replaced by "s," "b" by "q," and so on. To decode the message, the recipient needs to know the substitution pattern, or key. A trickier scheme is to use substitution and transposition. Transposition rearranges the letters in a word so that "chair" becomes "hciar," for example.

Another scheme is based on what is called "intersymbol dependence." Each letter in a word is replaced by another, depending upon the letter that, for example, preceded the one to be changed: a "u" becomes an "r" if preceded by a "b," a "y" if preceded by a "d," and so on. Extreme versions of this kind of coding might transform symbols depending upon a large number of letters that both preceded and followed the letter to be transformed.

By using various combinations of these three encryption schemes, it is possible to create as many different codes as we wish, and we can even tell everyone the "recipe" for creating the codes. But the recipe generates so many different codes that, for all practical purposes, no one would ever be able to discover the correct key. The situation is somewhat like a combination lock. Everyone may know how the lock works, but that is no help toward knowing the combination that opens a specific lock.

One particular encryption scheme invented by IBM generates about 10^{16} different codes. It would take a reasonably fast computer about three thousand years to search through all the possibilities. But some scientists fear that, given the rapid advance in computer technology, what takes thousands of years with present-day computers will someday take only seconds with future computers. So they suggest that the number of possible codes should be expanded to 10^{32}. This would increase the decoding time to about two-hundred-million, billion, billion times the estimated 15-billion-year age of the universe. Even with rapid advance in computer technology, it seems unlikely that such a code would be broken, even in the distant future.

The ability of computers to make and break codes is of interest to persons besides those concerned with their country's national security. We live in an age when computers have stored in their memories all sorts of information about individuals—their social security number, when and where they were born, their credit rating, how well they did in school, and many other personal details. It is very important that only authorized persons have access to these computerized files.

One way to protect the files is to require that the computer operator know a secret password. Without this password, no operator can gain access to the files. But as we know from many accounts in the newspapers, a password does not guarantee that unauthorized entry will be denied, since one computer can be used to search for another computer's password. Computer "hackers" just playing around with their computers have stumbled upon access to files that were supposedly well protected.

Another level of security is to encrypt the files, using one of the schemes we have just mentioned. No doubt future computers will have built-in special devices for encrypting messages so that files will be automatically coded. The irony of the situation, of course, is that the machines we use to encrypt can also be used "in reverse" for decryption. But the mathematics of coding theory suggests that it will always be more difficult to decrypt a message than to encrypt it. It's a little like hiding a needle in a haystack—the hiding is always easy compared to the finding.

The code-breaking procedure we've been discussing is a straightforward brute-force use of the computer; the computer simply inspects every possible solution until it finds the right one—if the number of possibilities is not too great. There are some situations, however, in which brute force can provide solutions in unexpected ways.

Let's suppose, for example, that we are given a map of an area that contains one island in an expanse of water. The map is square—10 miles on a side; so the total area of the map is 100 square miles. The problem is to find the area of the island, which, unfortunately, has a very irregular, complex shape.

We consider several possibilities: eyeball the map and guess at the area of the island, or perhaps decide that the island is roughly rectangular in shape and use the dimension

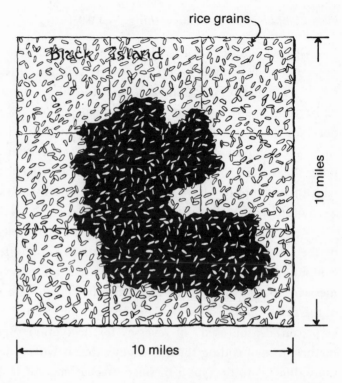

rice grains

Black Island

10 miles

10 miles

fig. 1

of the rectangle that approximates the size of the island to determine the area, and so on.

But then we notice a box of rice on a nearby shelf. We take a handful of rice and sprinkle the grains over the surface of the map, making certain that they are distributed randomly, as shown in Figure 1, with no clumps of rice here and there. Then we count the number of rice grains within the boundary of the island, and we also count the grains covering the water part of the map. It turns out that the island contains 330 grains of rice and the water 720 grains—a total of 1050 grains over the entire map.

We know at once that the land area of the map is less than the water area because there are fewer grains of rice on the island than on the water. And if we have done a good job of distributing the rice randomly, we can estimate the area of the island fairly well. It is 330/1050 of the total area of the map because the entire map is covered by 1050 grains of rice, 330 of which cover the island. Since the map contains 100 square miles, the area of the island is 330/1050 times 100 square miles, or about 31.4 square miles.

What has all this to do with a computer? Well, there are computer programs that generate random numbers. That is, the computer-produced numbers appear to have been drawn at random from a large bag full of numbers, so that we never know what number to expect next. We can use these random numbers in the computer program to simulate the scattering of rice on our map. That is, the random *numbers* can be converted to random *positions,* so as to simulate scattering rice on a map.

The map of the island can be introduced into the memory of the computer in one of several ways. In one technique, a scanning device attached to the computer enters the shape of the island into the computer as a string of numbers. Once the map is in the computer memory, we can "sprinkle" it with computer-generated "rice," using the random-number program. Then we can write another program to count the "rice grains" covering the island and surrounding water.

This method, the "Monte Carlo method," was invented during World War II and was used extensively in calculations concerning the design of the first atomic bomb. Here the problem was to determine how an atomic chain reaction developed, without actually setting off a bomb. Since a chain reaction is very random in nature, the Monte Carlo method is ideally suited to solving the problem. But this method obviously would not be feasible without fast computers doing millions of calculations in brute-force fashion.

There are other kinds of problems, seemingly simple, that require enormous computing time. One such problem involves building networks. As an illustration, let's consider the problem of connecting with telephone cables four cities located at the four corners of a square. An obvious and efficient-looking solution is shown in Figure 2A, where the cables leading from the four cities join in a junction box in the middle of the square. But this is not the best solution. Using two junction boxes connected by a cable and located in such a way that the angles formed by the cables at the junction boxes are precisely 120 degrees—as shown in Figure 2B—requires 3 percent less cable than the first solution. This may not seem like much improvement, but if the cities are hundreds of miles apart, and expensive cable must be laid in trenches, 3 percent could mean thousands of dollars in savings.

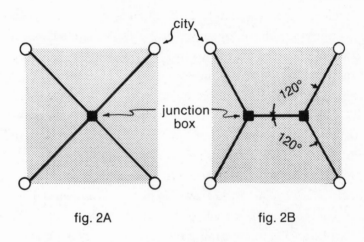

fig. 2A   fig. 2B

Designers of everything from computers to highway systems face these kinds of problems every day. In designing computers it is important that the components be wired together with the shortest possible paths because longer paths mean slower computers. And considering the enormous expenses of building and then maintaining highways, it is obvious why the shortest routes should be used whenever possible.

How do engineers and designers solve these kinds of network problems? One way is simply to model on a computer various possibilities, and hope that the best solution will appear. This is similar to brute-force searching through a set of codes to find the one that works, but there are important differences. In our decoding problem, we know when we have exhausted all the possibilities because we know the number of possibilities ahead of time. And when a message is successfully decoded, we know we have done the job correctly because only the correct solution gives a sensible message. But with the network problem—especially when a large number of components or terminals are involved—we are never certain that we have found the very best solution because any number of solutions may "make sense," and we don't know how many possible solutions should be inspected.

The problem of connecting cities or anything else we wish to connect by a network is one of the most celebrated in mathematics. Until 1961, it was not even known whether the best solution could be found. But then mathematicians discovered a systematic procedure for finding the best network. The trouble is that even today, with the fastest computers, networks involving 20 or more connecting points cannot be worked out within a reasonable time.

An even more difficult variation of the problem is that of the "traveling salesman." Suppose we have a salesman who needs to visit each of, say 50 cities once a year, and he must travel along existing roads. The question is, In what order should he visit the cities to minimize the number of miles he must drive?

A computer would have to search about 10^{65} routes to find the answer. And if the computer could investigate a million possible routes per second, it would take about 100 trillion-trillion-trillion-trillion years to complete the search.

All the types of problems we have discussed so far have one thing in common: we know how to solve them—it's just that the number of computations is so great that, in most cases, they are not practical to solve. But are there problems that no computer could ever solve, no matter how fast or how long it works?

One such problem was identified by Alan Turing, whom we met in Chapter 2. It revolves around a seemingly simple question: Is there any way for a computer always to know when it has completed a computation?—the "halting problem," as it is called.

As we know, Turing proved that the Universal Turing Machine could imitate any possible special-purpose computer. Today almost any programmable computer can be considered a Universal Turing Machine because it can be programmed to imitate any special-purpose machine. For example, we could program a computer to imitate a calculator. First the program would have to contain a description of the calculator—what functions it performs and how it performs them. Then we would have to feed the computer the data the calculator was to manipulate—perhaps a long string of numbers to be added, subtracted, multiplied, and divided.

Now it would be nice to include in our program another section that would *always* let the imitation calculator know when it had finished a computation or given a set of data. But can this be done? Surprisingly, the answer is no. It is not possible to find any procedure that will *always* work.

This is not a limitation of computers. Rather, it is a limitation that is "embedded" in the very nature of mathematical logic and is not subject to some clever solution. It is akin to the kind of law that says it is impossible to build a perpetual-motion machine. No matter how clever we are, we cannot get around such laws. Mathematicians have uncov-

ered a number of problems that cannot be solved. Most of
them have a kind of "self-referring" quality like the computer trying to decide whether it is through with its calculation or not.

Real computers, unlike Turing's abstract "paper" machines, must be built from real materials—copper, silicon,
plastic, and so on. So far we have considered two kinds of
limitations on computing—those calculations requiring so
many steps that they can't be carried out practically, and
those for which solutions are not mathematically possible.
Now we shall look at a different kind of problem—problems
whose solutions are beyond reach because of the finite nature
of the universe.

Many problems in mathematics have to do with whether
a statement is true or false. For example, consider the statement, For every number n there exists another number m,
such that m is less than $n + 1$. This is clearly a true statement because all we have to do is let $m = n$, and m will always automatically be less than $n + 1$. For example, if $n =
17$, then $n + 1 = 18$. So by letting $m = n$, or 17 in our exam-
ple, m will always be less than $n + 1$.

The truth or falsity of many statements in mathematics,
however, is not so easily seen as in our simple example, and
mathematicians have devoted great effort to developing methods for determining the truth or falsity of statements. In a
certain category of these statements, it has been possible to
prove that a procedure exists for determining their truth or
falsity. That is, we can write a computer program to determine the validity of all statements within this category. We
shall call this the "truth program," and our computer programmed with this program the "truth machine."

As we know, a computer consists of a large number of
AND, OR, and NOR gates. So we can think of a computer
programmed with the truth program as a specific arrange-

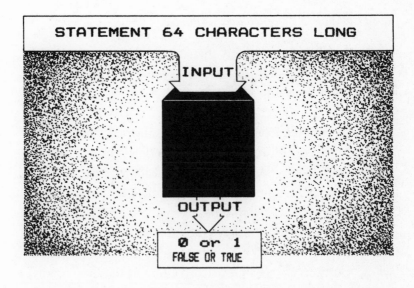

fig. 3   Truth machine

ment of gates. Figure 3 shows our truth machine schematically. First we have an input device that will accept mathematical statements up to 64 characters long. If the statement we wish to test is more than 64 characters long—including letters of the alphabet, numbers, and spaces—it cannot be handled by our truth machine. Inside the machine are AND, OR, and NOR gates connected according to the truth program. The output of the machine is very simple: a 0 or a 1. If the input statement is true, a 1 comes out; and if it is false, a 0 comes out.

Now mathematicians have been able to prove something very remarkable: to test the truthfulness of statements up to 64 characters long, the truth machine must have at least 10^{124} components inside. As we know, gates can be packed on computer chips by the thousands, but even so, each gate consists of thousands of atoms. And the atoms in turn are made up of protons and neutrons.

Let's suppose that technology has reached the point

where we can build a gate using just one proton or neutron—a very unlikely prospect. Then we would need at least 10^{124} protons and neutrons to build our truth machine.

How many protons and neutrons are there in the universe? Only around 10^{80}, according to the latest theories, which every day are receiving further confirmation from astronomical observations. In other words, the universe would have to contain about 1 (followed by 44 zeroes) as many protons and neutrons as we think it has to build just one truth machine!

So we see that some problems can't be solved because they take too long; others can't be solved because there is no solution; and still others can't be solved because there just isn't enough "stuff" in the universe to build a computer to solve them. Next we shall look at some limits placed on computers because the universe—and the laws that govern it—are the way they are.

13.
What's Ahead
for Computers?

"Knowledge is power," said the Romans, and we might add, "There is no knowledge without power." The Romans, of course, were speaking of political power, and we are speaking of the fact that information manipulation requires energy. A computer, like any other machine, cannot run without energy. It must be plugged into the nearest electrical outlet or have its own batteries.

We have seen that some problems can't be solved by a computer because there isn't enough material in the universe to build the computer. Is it possible, then, that are some problems that can't be solved simply because there is not enough energy?

Before we address this question, we need to consider two startling results from twentieth-century physics. The first came out of man's deeper understanding of the microworld— the world of atoms and electrons and the dozens of other particles that seem to be the building blocks of the universe. This deeper understanding, called *quantum physics,* revealed that the faster we wish to do something, the more energy it takes to do it. This fact has a direct application to computers, for the faster we want them to compute, the more energy they take. Increased computation speed requires that the gates and memory banks in the computer respond more rapidly, and this increases energy demand.

More specifically, quantum physics says that for a given amount of energy, E, the information flow in bits-per-second in the computer cannot be more than E divided by a number called *Plank's constant,* after the physicist who discovered it, usually designated by the letter h. Plank's constant shows up in many equations in physics. Stated mathematically, the flow of energy in a computer in bits-per-second is never any faster than E/h. If we let I stand for the information flow in bits-per-second, then we can write our equation as $I = E/h$, which gives the maximum rate at which information can flow in a computer. We shall return to this point shortly.

The second result we need from twentieth-century physics is probably the most famous equation in modern science: $E = mc^2$—the basic equation that led to development of the atomic bomb. Einstein's literally earth-shaking equation says that energy, E, and mass, m, are interchangeable, and that the ratio of the interchange is the speed of light, c, multiplied by itself. Since the speed of light is such a big number— 186,000 miles per second, it is easy to see from the equation why such a small amount of matter produces such an enormous amount of energy—the energy that is the basis not only of atomic bombs but of nuclear power plants and the seemingly endless supply of energy from the sun.

Let's bring our two equations, $I = E/h$ and $E = mc^2$, together now. We'll imagine that our computer has a certain amount of mass, m, available to it that can be converted to energy according to Einstein's equation. Then the maximum information flow rate for our computer is $I = E/h = mc^2/h$, where we have simply substituted the value mc^2 for E, in our equation for I.

For example, if we had a mass of about 1 divided by

10^{43} ounces of mass to convert to energy, we could have an information flow of about one million bits per second. In other words, the tiniest amount of mass, converted to energy, provides a very large flow of information.

Suppose now that we imagine that the total mass of the universe is available for conversion to energy to run our computer, and that the entire time the universe has existed, up to the present time, has been available for calculation. Are there any problems for which this would not be enough time and energy to reach a solution?

Yes! Even some problems that do not at first look very difficult. This would not be enough time and energy to compute all the possible positions in a chess game, for instance, or to find the shortest route in the traveling salesman problem involving a large number of cities. The situation is actually somewhat more demanding than what we have described because we have assumed that *all* of the energy would be available for transmitting and manipulating information; but no devices are 100 percent efficient, so some of the energy would simply disappear as heat.

We are becoming used to living in a world of limited resources—limited space, food, fresh water, fossil fuels, and so forth. So perhaps we should not be surprised that lack of energy and time restrict our computational capabilities. What may be more surprising is the almost infinite complexity of chess games and traveling salesmen's problems when viewed in the context of our computational abilities.

In this discussion we have treated computers as energy-using machines, which for all practical purposes they are. Some scientists, however, argue that computers could be built to process information without using energy. If this is true, then computers would not be machines in the normal sense of the word and would therefore not be subject to the constraints we have considered here. But the matter is far from settled; and for now, at least, the "perpetual motion" computer is at best another paper computer, like the Turing machine, that serves as a focus for heated debate.

Another basic limit on our ability to compute has to do with the finite speed with which signals travel. Here we turn again to Einstein. According to his famous "Special Theory of Relativity," no signal can travel faster than the speed of light, 186,000 miles per second. Put another way, in one-billionth of a second (1 nanosecond), light travels about 1 foot.

Suppose we had a computer whose electronic switches could open and close in as short a time as 10 nanoseconds. Then the switches should never be more than 10 feet apart; otherwise, a switch would have to wait between openings and closings for a signal telling it "what to do next." Future computers will have switches that operate as fast as 10 times per nanosecond. So in principle, at least, such a computer should fit into a volume less than 2 inches in diameter for the finite speed of the signal not to be a limiting factor.

One of the most powerful computers in the world, the CRAY-1, has a circular structure to keep wiring distances to a minimum. The whole computer occupies about 8 square feet of floor space, with a dozen cupboard-like units surrounding an open core. Packing all the necessary circuitry into such a small space created a huge problem—how to keep the circuitry from overheating. The problem was solved by embedding in the circuitry a system of cooling coils connected to a massive Freon gas cooling unit below the computer.

The CRAY-1's successor, the CRAY-2, contains no wires longer than 16 inches, compared to some of its predecessor's 4-foot wires; and the entire CPU rests in a glass "aquarium" about 26 inches high, 38 inches long, and 24 inches wide filled with liquid fluorocarbon to keep it cool. This com-

puter will perform more than 1 billion operations per second, and curiously enough, does not use the latest technology. Its designer, Seymour Cray, believes that it is best to use older, more reliable technology rather than the latest unproven technology. He credits the great speed of his computers to the "unique packaging" that allows him to pack time-proven circuits into small volumes.

Future computers may run at temperatures near absolute zero, or −479.6 degrees Fahrenheit, for two important reasons. First, the cooler the environment in which the computer is situated, the less power it needs to run. This is because the tiny signals that flow around inside the computer fluctuate in strength, and the hotter the environment of the computer, the greater the fluctuation. If the fluctuations are

The Cray-1 at the National Center for Atmospheric Research, in Boulder, Colorado, is one of the most powerful computers in the world.

too great, the signals are so "noisy" that the various components in the computer can no longer interpret the meanings of the signals. The only alternative is to increase the signal strength to overcome the noise, which means increasing the power input to the computer—and this in turn makes the computer run hotter.

The second reason for operating at temperatures near absolute zero is that this makes it possible to use a new kind of switch called the *Josephson junction,* which operates only at very low temperatures. The Josephson junction has two big advantages: it can open and close in a few trillionths of a second, and it takes very little energy to operate—about one one-thousandth of the energy it takes to operate a transistor switch in today's computers.

This high-speed switching and miserly energy consumption go hand in hand. At such high switching rates, the computer needs to be very small, since the signal travels at the speed of light—about one one-thousandth of a foot in a trillionth of a second. If we had millions of transistors packed into such small volumes, the heat generated by normal electrical components would cause the tiny computer to melt itself down. The Josephson junction is at present a long way from being a practical reality in computers, but most scientists believe that it—or something akin to it—will be a practical reality in the 1990s.

In Chapter 5 we described the chip-making process whereby circuits are reduced photographically. It appears that this technology will be adequate for the next decade or so. Some experts believe that the billion-transistor chip will be a reality by the turn of the century. Still scientists continue to explore other technologies. One approach that has received considerable attention is the use of microscopic magnetic bubbles. The bubbles can be moved around electronically for computation and memory storage. One advantage of the bubbles is that they retain their positions after the computer is turned off. That is, a computer memory based on magnetic bubbles would not be lost, as it is with RAM, when the power to the computer is interrupted.

Another technology suggests the possibility of using laser beams to record vast amounts of information on disks similar in size to LP records. The laser beam produces microscopic pits or other distortions on the smooth, hard disk that can later be detected and "read" by another laser beam in a playback device. This technology has already been applied commercially in video disk players that attach to TV sets to provide movies or other prerecorded material. Present indications are that one or two million pages of material could be stored on one such disk—compared to about 200 pages on

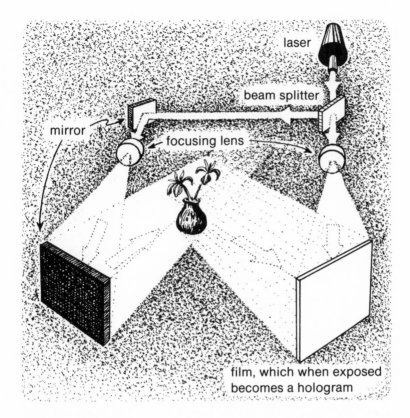

laser

beam splitter

mirror

focusing lens

film, which when exposed
becomes a hologram

fig. 1

a floppy disk with present technology. An entire encyclopedia, including pictures, would easily fit on a single disk;
and the blank disks, when mass produced, would probably
cost only a few dollars each.

Another kind of optical storage is based on holography.
The principle of holography was worked out in the 1940s,
but it had to await the invention of the laser to become a
practical reality. Holography is best known as the basis for
projecting lifelike, three-dimensional images into space. A
"hologram," the piece of film on which the image is stored,
is created by using the arrangement shown in Figure 1. Light
from a laser is split into two beams. One beam travels di-

rectly to the film, and the other is diverted by mirrors to the object, where it is reflected by the object back toward the film. The two beams combine at the film to produce a complex image that is recorded permanently on the film as the hologram.

When we look at the hologram we do not see an image of flowers in a vase, but a piece of exposed film with varying patterns of light and dark. From an information point of view, the process is somewhat similar to coding a word or a book into bits of information. If we look at the pattern of bits, they are completely meaningless; yet this meaningless pattern contains the same information as the original word or book. In the same sense, the hologram contains all of the

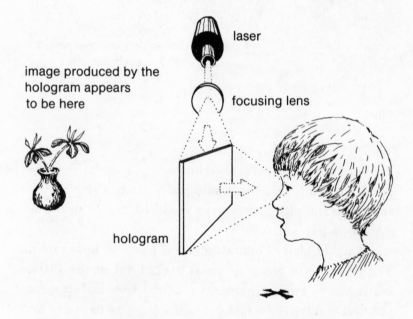

laser

image produced by the
hologram appears
to be here

focusing lens

hologram

fig. 2   Viewer does not see the hologram at all, but looking through it sees only the vase, seemingly suspended in space. A viewer at X, also looking through the hologram, would see a slightly different view of the three-dimensional image.

information necessary to reconstruct the original image—in this case, the flowers in a vase.

The reconstruction process is shown in Figure 2. When we shine a laser beam on the hologram, a three-dimensional figure appears "in thin air," in the same position as that occupied by the original image. This is a true three-dimensional figure, which we can walk around, seeing one side of the vase and then the other.

There are many ways in which information can be recorded by using holography, but we shall give just one simple illustration. Suppose the vase is replaced by a checkerboard, and in some of the squares we have marked 1's and in others, 0's. These 1's and 0's might represent a few words or perhaps a simple equation. The hologram of the checkerboard would then contain the same information as the checkerboard itself, but in a different form. To recover the information we would, as before, illuminate the hologram with a laser, producing an image of the checkerboard in space. Using something like this arrangement, it is possible to store more than 100 million bits of information on one 4 by 6-inch piece of film. And optical readers have been built that can recover information from holographic images at rates as high as several million bits per second.

One of the amazing properties of the hologram is that each point in it contains information about the entire image and contributes this information to create the "image in space" effect. That is, each point helps to define and reinforce the image produced by each of the other points, and the greater the number of points, the clearer the image. Because of this characteristic, if we cut a hologram in two, we could still recover the complete image by illuminating just the hologram fragment; the image would be less clearly defined because fewer points would be contributing to it, but it would all be there. From a practical standpoint, this means that dust and scratches on a hologram do not frustrate our attempts to recover its information—a situation that can present problems in some other systems.

The new technologies we have been discussing, amazing as they are, are still based on conventional materials—silicon, copper, photographic film, and so forth. Yet computers in nature—from the earthworm's brain on up—are based on complex organic molecules that contain carbon and hydrogen and oxygen and other elements. This fact has led many scientists to wonder whether future computers may not be built from similar materials; instead of silicon chips, we would have "biochips." Biologists already know how to harness bacteria to produce complex hormones and insulin. And if living creatures can reproduce, why not computers that build new computers by the millions?

The size of individual components in chips has already reached biological building-block dimensions—smaller than the human red blood cell, for example. But still there are many problems to overcome. No one has any good ideas about how to connect molecule-size switches or how to build molecules with on-off properties. And even if we knew how to build them and connect them, we know very little about how they should be arranged to function efficiently and effectively.

Today's computers, as we have pointed out, perform one task at a time. But the human brain seems to handle many tasks simultaneously. This notion of performing many tasks at the same time is called "parallel processing" by computer scientist, and the computers in the 1990s will probably be of the parallel processing variety.

But this prospect poses new problems. How do we program such computers, making certain that the many tasks being performed at the same time all "come together" at the right time and that what is going on in one part of the computer doesn't interfere with what is going on in another part? Parallel-processing computers represent enormous organizational problems; but nature seems to have found a solution, so perhaps we can, too.

In the final chapter of our book we shall explore the subject of artificial intelligence, or AI, as computer scientists call it. Scientists studying AI are very much concerned with questions of organization and memory capacity and speed of operation. And most interesting of all, the question: will machines someday think, be creative, and have feelings? If these things come true, how will computers be integrated into society? Some people are already saying that these prospects are so frightening that computers shouldn't have a future at all. But others view the prospects as challenging and exciting, with potential for great and good results.

14.
Can Computers Think?

Tell me where is fancy bred,
Or in the heart, or in the head?

The opening lines of Bassanio's song in Shakespeare's *The Merchant of Venice* summarize a debate that has been going on ever since man began to wonder about his intelligence: what is it and where does it reside? Plato thought the seat of intelligence was in the brain, but Aristotle argued for the heart.

Today we universally associate intelligence with the brain. But some experts in the field of Artificial Intelligence—the attempt to mimic and understand the human brain with computers—say that intellect cannot be isolated from the body. The way we think and feel about ourselves, they say, very much depends upon the fact that we breathe, smell the flowers, walk with two legs, compose music to be played by two hands, see the world through two eyes, and so on. It is not a question of mind and body, they say, but rather an integrated whole, where mind and body are a convenient concept invented by man as a way of understanding his nature.

Can computers think? This frequently-posed question usually sets off a multitude of arguments. One position is that thinking is more than mere computation—that no computer will ever be able to take the place of the brain because human beings possess some essence that is beyond the material universe. Others argue that the brain is subject to the same laws of nature that govern atoms and galaxies, and that there is no need to look to some mysterious essence to explain intelligence. The universe, they say, and the rules it obeys, will ultimately prove sufficient to unravel the mystery of intellect.

Of course, the biggest problem with trying to answer the question: Can computers think? is that no one really knows what thinking is. So how would we know whether a computer was thinking or not? Alan Turing got around this problem to some extent by posing the question in a different way. He imagined a scene something like the following, although in his original discussion there were three persons instead of just two:

A room is divided into two areas by a partition that blocks anyone who is sitting on one side from seeing who or what is on the other side. The two areas are connected by a cable over which messages can pass. A terminal consisting of a keyboard and a CRT display screen is attached to each end of the cable. Any message typed on one side of the partition appears on the screen on the other side. With this arrangement, two persons sitting on either side of the partition can communicate.

Now Turing posed the following problem: suppose you are sitting on one side of the partition carrying on a conversation with the other side. The question is: are you conversing with another person or with a computer? Turing suggests that if you can think of no question that will resolve the issue, then for all practical purposes it doesn't make any difference whether you are talking to a computer or to a person.

This test, now called the Turing test, bypasses many of the philosophical and metaphysical difficulties concerning intelligence because it faces the question in a rather matter-of-fact way: if you can't tell whether you are talking to a computer or a human being, what difference does it make? But then, we may not feel that this simplistic position fits all occasions. It's hard to imagine composing sonnets or writing a symphony for a computer. Or even telling it a joke. A sense of humor is considered one important characteristic of intelligence.

From the earliest days of computers, many persons realized that computers could be an important tool in education, particularly in automating routine activities. Flash cards used to teach such basics as word recognition and the multiplication tables are a good example. Computers can be programmed to display "electronic flash cards" on CRT screens, and the pupil's response can be monitored by the computer so that it will continually come back with misspelled words or numbers whose sums or products the pupil often misses.

Of course, this is an example of something we have mentioned before—using new technology, at first, to carry out something that formerly had been done in a less efficient, more laborious way. But then people began to think about the possibility of going beyond electronic flash cards. Perhaps some of the ideas about how people learn could be tested and augmented on computers. And furthermore, if we can learn something about the way people learn, then maybe this knowledge could be used to teach computers to learn.

Many attempts have been made in this direction, but we shall mention only one. The Swiss psychologist Jean Piaget developed some theories suggesting how small children learn. One of his principal conclusions, based on many years of observation, is that children learn by doing and by thinking about what they are doing. That is, children do not learn everything by memorizing facts or by watching others; rather, small children construct theories as to how the world operates, and then continuously adjust their theories as required by their actual experience with the world.

A programming language called LOGO has been strongly influenced by Piaget's convictions. LOGO attempts to provide a bridge between abstract reasoning and actual experience. In many programming languages, such as BASIC, the programmer must expend considerable effort if he wishes to create new instructions in addition to BASIC's predetermined operations such as INPUT, GOTO, and so forth, as we discussed in Chapter 6. In LOGO, the programmer has greater liberty to create his own operations and commands to suit his own interests and needs.

Another important characteristic of LOGO is that the programmer can often see the results of his commands graphically, which is one example of how abstract ideas are turned into concrete realities. To illustrate, let's consider a simple LOGO program that tells the computer to draw a square on the CRT. The first line of the program is TO SQUARE.

This line tells the computer that we are creating a new operation called "SQUARE," but we haven't yet told it what "SQUARE" means. We do this in the second line of the program: REPEAT 4 [FORWARD 50 RIGHT 90].

The last part of this cryptic instruction in LOGO tells the computer that "SQUARE" means, partially, "Trace a line by moving 50 spaces forward along the screen and then turn right at a 90-degree angle." An equivalent instruction for someone standing in a field would be "Walk 50 paces in

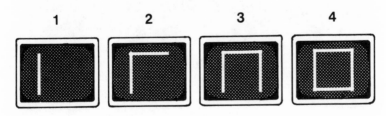

fig. 1

a straight line and then turn right at a right angle." The first part of the instruction, REPEAT 4, means "Repeat the last part of the instruction [FORWARD 50 RIGHT 90] four times." As Figure 1 shows, the result of repeating the last part of the instruction four times is a square.

The last statement of the program is END, which tells the computer, as seems reasonable, that there are no more instructions in the program. Our entire program looks like this:

```
TO SQUARE
REPEAT 4 [FORWARD 50 RIGHT 90]
END
```

Now when we give our computer the instruction SQUARE, it draws a square on the screen. Other instructions in LOGO allow us to change the size of the square easily, without defining other operations for each size square

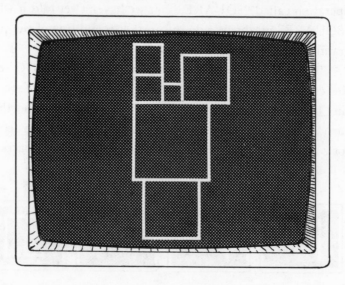

fig. 2

we want. And still other operations allow us to put different size squares together in different arrangements, to form, for example, the stack of blocks shown in Figure 2.

We can also define other commands that allow us to draw circles and triangles and almost any other shape we want. With this versatility, we can create our own electronic "erector set," whose components, of our own choosing, can be arranged in almost any way we please, as shown in Figure 3.

One of the interesting things about LOGO is that it is "noncritical." That is, if we wish to call a square a circle, that's all right with LOGO. We are at liberty to name our commands anything we like, even though they are not according to customary conventions. This means that children can create commands to draw shapes whose names they do not know—perhaps a trapezoid or a pentagon—and they can call the shape any name they like. Later on, someone might say, "Oh, your program draws pentagons," or octagons, or whatever. And at this point the child discovers that there is a

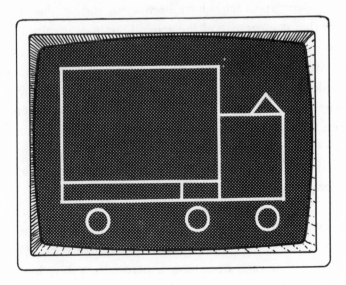

fig. 3

name for the shape he has created, and thus he adds to his vocabulary and store of knowledge.

We have only scratched the surface of things that can be done with LOGO—things like creating video games or writing music. The significant point about LOGO—in contrast to electronic flash cards, for instance—is that the computer is no longer simply a tool for instruction, but a tool for exploring and creating. Even so, interesting as LOGO is, it is still a tool whose designs are no better than the hand that guides the tool.

One of man's abilities that sets him apart from the rest of nature is his ability to create. Chimpanzees and dolphins, no matter how smart they seem to be, don't write great symphonies, produce inspiring art, or understand the universe through mathematical masterpieces like the General Theory of Relativity. But if creativity is beyond the reach of chimpanzees and dolphins, is it beyond the reach of computers? For some years we have heard about poems or music composed by computers. How do computers do these things?

Many approaches have been used, and we shall explore one that is suggestive of the general methods involved. As we know, computers are good at analyzing great quantities of information. It is no trick to program a computer to analyze in detail Mozart's compositions—or those of any other composer. The computer can search out the common themes that run through Mozart's music and compile this information in the form of statistical tables that tell, for example, what note is likely to follow another or what rhythms run throughout Mozart's music.

Now let's suppose that we use this statistical information to create a Mozart sonata. What we require is that the music sound like Mozart from a statistical point of view. We don't require that each note have a particular value, but rather that the composition as a whole should sound as though it came from Mozart's hand. This statistical constraint, rather than a note-by-note constraint, allows the computer to compose a "Mozart sonata" that is not an exact replica of an existing Mozart sonata, but which nevertheless sounds like Mozart. Mozart, yes—but not *great* Mozart, according to the experts who have listened to such music.

Is this creativity? It is probably true that this second-rate "computer Mozart" is better than the music written by the average person—or even second-rate Mozarts. So where does this leave us?

Well, probably in the same situation we found ourselves when we asked the question: can computers think? Since we really don't know what thinking is, the question cannot be answered satisfactorily. And since we don't know the mechanism of creativity, we don't know whether our computer-composed music has anything to do with the way the brain creates music or not.

One of the basic methods of modern science is to attempt to understand the universe in terms of basic forces and building blocks—protons, neutrons, electrical and gravitational forces, and so on. Many complicated phenomena can be analyzed and understood at four different levels. Let's consider a computer and its program as an example.

At the lowest level, level one, we have transistors. We can think of this as the building-block level. Next, at the second level, we have mechanisms such as AND and OR gates built from transistors. And then at the third level we have detailed, step-by-step procedures called *algorithms* that, when converted to a program, instruct computers composed of gates to perform certain computations. At this level a particular algorithm always yields a specific result for a specific input. If it is a "square-root" algorithm, for example, then when the input is 4, the output is always ± 2.

The highest level, the theoretical level, is not concerned

with specific details of how something is carried out. At this level we are more concerned with the *theory* of what is being done and what can be done. As a simple example, we might wonder—if we were primitive man—whether numbers could be multiplied and divided. We are not concerned with whether we are to use Arabic or Roman numerals, but just with the theoretical possibility of multiplying and dividing *any* numbers. Once we are sure something could be done at the theoretical level, then we could be assured that we would not be wasting our time and energy looking for a specific multiplying or division procedure—or algorithm—whether for Arabic or Roman numerals or any other number system.

We can make a similar analysis of intelligence. At the lowest level we have the building blocks in the brain—the neurons, synapses, and so forth. This is the physiological level, and its mechanisms are pretty well understood.

At the next level we have the mechanisms for memory, for example, which are in some ways related to the interconnections of the neurons. As we move to successively higher levels, our understanding grows ever more uncertain. At the third level we know next to nothing about how the brain carries out what it needs to do—the specific algorithms it employs to give us the "feeling" that we see the world through our eyes, for example.

Our understanding of the top level, the theoretical level, is essentially a blank page. For example, one of the things the brain does is interpret and fill in pieces of information where information is missing—and it often does this without our knowing it. Figure 4 shows a Necker cube, named for the Swiss naturalist L. A. Necker, who invented it. Here we have the representation of a three-dimensional figure, a cube, on a two-dimensional surface—the paper. We know rationally that the cube is not three dimensional; yet it appears to our "mind's eye" to be so.

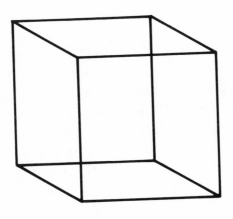

fig. 4 Necker's cube

Furthermore, as we stare at the cube it seems to flip back and forth between two different configurations. That is, this particular two-dimensional representation of a three-dimensional object is interpreted by the brain in two different ways; and the brain, in trying to interpret and fill in missing information—so as to turn a two-dimensional object into a three-dimensional object—comes up with two possible solutions, settling on neither one.

This kind of phenomenon is certainly involved with the upper levels of processing in the brain, and not the lower, building-block level. At the building-block level, the brain is dealing with the actual signals that are "input" through the eyes into the brain. These signals do not flip back and forth; they are constant and are directly related to the light reflected into our eyes by the figure we are examining.

Necker's cube is a very good illustration that the brain interprets the information fed to it and that we are always in the position of not seeing things as they "really are," but as they are filtered through the upper processing levels of the brain.

As we said, our understanding of the building blocks of the brain is fairly complete, but we have seen that this has been very little help in understanding what intelligence is. We are somewhat in the position of someone looking into a cabinet filled with a maze of transistors, capacitors, and resistors connected by thousands of wires. We recognize the transistors, capacitors, and resistors, and we understand how they work; and yet we have no idea what function this cabinet full of tangled parts performs. And until we understand what problems the brain has to solve, at the highest theoretical level, to provide us with emotions, creativity, judgment, or whatever, we will not be likely to make much sense out of what the "beehive" of activity in the brain is all about.

It is a characteristic of man to attempt to understand his nature in terms of the level of his present technology. Descartes imagined that nerves transmitted signals like tiny mechanical machines. In the first decade of this century, the nervous system was understood as a vast telephone network, with the brain playing the part of the central switching box. Now the brain is compared to the computer. But we know that the brain is not like most of today's computers because the brain performs many functions at the same time. As we suggested in the previous chapter, however, computers of the future will be parallel-processing computers; so to this extent the computer begins to look more like the brain.

Yet there are some curious things that make computers seem quite different from the brain. We explained how the finite speed of light limits the computation speed of computers. In electronic circuits, impulses are made up of electrons that travel near the speed of light, whereas the signal carriers in the brain are much heavier sodium and potassium ions that travel at a leisurely 60 miles per hour.

We are rapidly approaching the point where we will be able to pack more information into a skull-sized cavity than the brain now stores. And we know that the switches in the brain are "almost" switches, not "on-off" switches like those in a computer. So speed, high memory density, and precision switches are not enough to account for intelligence. And even if we succeed in building biochips and biocomputers, we are not guaranteed that we will have "brain-like" computers because the uniqueness of the brain may be more a question of how its parts are connected than the matter they are made of.

It is common practice to measure man's handiwork against nature's, with the assumption that nature represents perfection. So will the ultimate computer resemble the brain? Maybe, maybe not. Nature may have already traced out the present course of man's brain and found it adequate to meet her needs—and the needs of man. If man were smart enough— or stupid enough—to build a computer that could "outthink" his brain, he might be doomed. Then again, if he were smart enough to do this, he should also be smart enough to manage his invention intelligently. Maybe nature's plans include all this, or maybe she hasn't thought of it yet. And maybe we'll never know.

GLOSSARY

Analog Computer—A computer that is constructed so as to imitate the system or process of interest.

Algorithm—A procedure for solving a problem that involves a finite number of steps.

Assembly Language—A computer language that interacts directly with the computer hardware.

BASIC—A high-level programming language that stands for Beginner's All-purpose Symbolic Instruction Code.

Binary—Describes a system in which each element can take on only one of two values—a 0 or a 1, for example.

Bit—The smallest unit of information, usually represented by a 0 or a 1.

Bug—Any error in a program.

Bus—The communication path over which information flows inside a computer.

Byte—Eight bits of information.

Chip—An electronic circuit made by etching thousands of transistors and other components on a wafer of silicon a fraction of an inch on a side.

CPU—Stands for Central Processing Unit, the part of the computer that carries out the arithmetic and logical operations.

Digital Computer—A computer that uses on-off electrical pulses (bits) to perform calculations and logical operations.

Exponent—A shorthand method for indicating how many times a number is to be multiplied by itself. For example, 10^3 means $10 * 10 * 10$; 3 is the exponent.

High-level Language—A programming language, such as BASIC, which has some of the characteristics of natural language but which is precise enough for programming a computer.

Hologram—A piece of film that, when illuminated by a laser, produces a 3-dimensional image in space.

Input/output—An input device, such as a keyboard, feeds information to a computer. An output device, such as a printer, displays information generated by the computer. Input and output are also used as verbs; one can "input" data by using a keyboard.

Laser—A device that produces light at a single frequency rather than at many frequencies as do most light sources such as incandescent bulbs and candles.

LISP—A programming language that is particularly suited for programming computer-controlled robots or writing programs to simulate artificial intelligence.

LOGO—A programming language that allows the user to define his own commands. The language is especially useful in helping children to learn programming concepts.

Microprocessor—A chip that contains a complete CPU.

Model—The part of a program that simulates a process or system via equations and logical relationships.

Machine Language—The binary language the computer uses to carry out its operations.

Program—A set of instructions that tells the computer what to do.

RAM—Stands for Random Access Memory, and refers to temporary memory storage in a computer in which information can be both stored and taken from very quickly.

ROM—Stands for Read Only Memory, and refers to permanent memory storage in a computer from which information can only be taken but not stored.

I N D E X